real girls serving a real GOD

An Invitation for Women of All Ages to Trade Busyness and Perfectionism for an Authentic Life Rooted in God's Hope and Truth

DR. TERI COX-MEADOWS

LIFEWISE BOOKS

REAL GIRLS SERVING A REAL GOD

An Invitation for Women of All Ages to Trade Busyness and Perfectionism for an Authentic Life Rooted in God's Hope and Truth

By Teri Cox-Meadows Ed.D.

Copyright © 2021 Teri Cox-Meadows Ed.D. All rights reserved. Except for brief quotations for review purposes, no part of this book may be reproduced in any form without prior written permission from the author

All scriptures came from biblegateway.com and are ESV unless otherwise noted.

Scriptures marked CSB are taken from The Christian Standard Bible. Copyright © 2017 by Holman Bible Publishers. Used by permission. Christian Standard Bible®, and CSB® are federally registered trademarks of Holman Bible Publishers, all rights reserved.

THE HOLY BIBLE, ENGLISH STANDARD VERSION (ESV): Scriptures taken from THE HOLY BIBLE, ENGLISH STANDARD VERSION ® Copyright© 2001 by Crossway, a publishing ministry of Good News Publishers. Used by permission.

Scriptures marked KJV are taken from the KING JAMES VERSION (KJV): KING JAMES VERSION, public domain.

Scriptures marked NIV are taken from the NEW INTERNATIONAL VERSION (NIV): Scripture taken from THE HOLY BIBLE, NEW INTERNATIONAL VERSION ®. Copyright© 1973, 1978, 1984, 2011 by Biblica, Inc.™. Used by permission of Zondervan.

Scriptures marked NKJV are taken from the NEW KING JAMES VERSION (NKJV): Scripture taken from the NEW KING JAMES VERSION®. Copyright© 1982 by Thomas Nelson, Inc. Used by permission. All rights reserved.

Scriptures marked NASB are taken from the NEW AMERICAN STANDARD BIBLE®, copyright© 1960, 1962, 1963, 1968, 1971, 1972, 1973, 1975, 1977, 1995 by The Lockman Foundation. Used by permission.

Scripture quotations marked MSG are taken from THE MESSAGE, copyright © 1993, 2002, 2018 by Eugene H. Peterson. Used by permission of NavPress. All rights reserved. Represented by Tyndale House Publishers, Inc.

Published by:

LIFEWISE BOOKS

PO BOX 1072
Pinehurst, TX 77362
LifeWiseBooks.com

To contact the author: coxconsulting.org

ISBN (Print): 978-1-952247-58-3
ISBN (Ebook): 978-1-952247-59-0

Dedication

I would like to dedicate this work to everyone who has contemplated their faith and its depth at some point as well as everyone who has lost something or someone they deeply loved. I hope you are stronger because of the journey, and if you are not yet, that you will find strength within these pages.

Acknowledgements

First and foremost, I thank God for His redemption stories in my life. I also want to thank Bryan K. Meadows, who has given me new laughter; I see you...

I am beyond grateful to my church families who have crafted me over the years, ReNew Community Church, Cabot; you are my tribe. Marshall Road Baptist, you carried me through the valley - thanks is not enough. The Church at Rock Creek - I grew and learned to love through you.

Lastly, I want to thank my sisters, whom I laugh and grow up with-still, and my friends who have given more support and joy than I can say. I have also been gifted with some of the greatest friends in the world and I cannot be who I am without you. There are too many to name, but if you are part of my inner circle, you know me, and I love you. To my mentors who have helped shape my life - may God pour out abundance upon you and yours.

To my Daddy and my Pappa, my love for you is unwavering; our journeys have not always been easy, but you are forever mine, and I am oh, so glad.

May God protect and bless all who read these pages. We have prayed for you.

Contents

INTRODUCTION ... 1

CHAPTER 1
Can You Imagine? ... 3

CHAPTER 2
Girl Tribe ... 21

CHAPTER 3
When Life Stops, Where Do We Fall? ... 31

CHAPTER 4
Staying Positive in a Negative Space ... 43

CHAPTER 5
Learning Discipline Takes Discipline ... 59

CHAPTER 6
Love...It's Complicated ... 71

CHAPTER 7
The Flesh Wants: Living in My Spirit Instead of My Feels ... 91

CHAPTER 8
Courage to Fight for the Good and Wisdom to Know
What Good Means ... 107

CHAPTER 9
Do Prayers Really Matter? ... 119

CHAPTER 10
Powerful Love ... 135

CHAPTER 11
Chasing Down Hope   147

CHAPTER 12
Choose Kind Words   161

CHAPTER 13
Listening Takes Patience   177

CHAPTER 14
A Scarlet Thread Leads to Redemption   189

CONCLUSION
Author's Notes   205

ABOUT THE AUTHOR: 209

ENDNOTES   211

Introduction

The more I study and write about communication, servant leadership, and prayer, the more there is for me to pray about. The more I look into the eyes of women in the Bible, whom some in academia say are mostly insignificant characters, the more I find significance for my own journey through life.

I have divided *Real Girls Serving a Real God* into chapters with a glimpse into the lives of lesser-known women in the Bible mixed with stories from my own life. Each chapter is set in a way that I hope will make these women's stories shine through by examining them in ways we may never have considered before.

Each chapter contains five sections:

> **REAL LIFE:** a story from my journey through heartache and healing.
>
> **REAL WOMEN FROM SCRIPTURE:** a story from my mind's eye, study, and reflection upon lesser-known women or rarely considered viewpoints of women in scripture.

REAL BATTLES: a glimpse at authentic issues we, as women, struggle with and face in our daily lives.

REAL POWER FOR THE REAL WORLD: a reminder or teaching on how we can use instruction from God to overcome the battles.

GET REAL - REFLECTION & PRAYER: seven reflection questions based upon the ideas and themes of each chapter and a short prayer. I encourage you to buy a beautiful, fresh journal, and use it to answer and reflect on the questions found in this section.

I pray that the lessons, challenges and victories interwoven between the stories of these lesser-known women as well as my own will help you consider your own narrative. I hope you will understand which lessons you still need to learn or share with others. I may introduce ideas that are new; this is explained later in Chapter One. I do not perceive this as an academic scholarly work, but as one of God-filled imagination intertwined with stories that will make us all grapple with our views and grow.

I invite everyone to measure my words against the Bible. Each of us has an obligation to test words against the Word. I Thessalonians 5:21 expects Christians to measure what they read and hear. Hold what makes you think and let it lead you toward sustainable change.

I pray a blessing of new roots and dreams surrounded by healing and hope for each one of us as we get real with ourselves and the Holy Spirit.

CHAPTER 1

Can You Imagine?

"And I am sure of this, that he who began a good work in you will bring it to completion at the day of Jesus Christ."
(Philippians 1:6)

REAL LIFE: We Are Not Done Yet

My work often centers around understanding various and sometimes oppositional viewpoints. If you were near me for any length of time, you might hear me say, "Let's look at that from another perspective," or "Let's take a 360-degree view." Simply put, this means, "Can we look at this issue from as many angles as possible; 360 degrees around the problem?" In my experience, there are usually more than two sides of every story.

As a note on my background, I am the owner of a few businesses, the founder of a nonprofit, and I have served as part of a church plant staff for several years. My working and serving adventures look different every day. In the business world, I am an executive coach, a communication and leadership trainer, a keynote speaker, a professional development provider, and a health and wellness networker and coach.

In the faith-based world, you might find me speaking at a women's conference, coaching pastors and church leaders, ministering to broken folks, talking with teens, walking alongside widows or anyone struggling with grief, writing, or singing. I am sad to say this was not always the case. There were years when I pushed God out of my life and years when I just did not walk with a like-minded faith tribe. Despite my wanderings, my faith became my own in the midst of my troubles.

As a child, I watched my grandparents devoutly serve and my parents struggle to give up worldly desires. Even in hard, dark places, I studied religions, read doctrines, and found God's light for myself. I chose Jesus because I have seen His fingerprint on my life. My stories of change and choice follow within these pages. Some of them are ugly and raw, but all of it is real.

My close friends say you could not make up the things that have happened in my life. The events in my life have been both tragic and triumphant, but my hope is that you will come to understand that God has always been with me, even when I could not see Him. I pray you will grasp the fact that He has always been with you, too. The primary reason why I chose to write and share is to help others know God is real. I know it because I have seen it, read it, and lived it.

As a child and teen, I found myself in the middle of pandemonium much of the time. I used reading and my imagination to take me away from my real life and into places I could only envision. Imagination can be used for good or evil. While Silly Putty was a happy accident by a scientist looking to make a cheap synthetic rubber product for use during World War II, most inventions are not accidents.[1] They are imagined first.

Imagination is the creator of invention and grand adventure. When we let it run wild and do not harness the bad, blatantly wrong, or evil things we imagine, imagination can cause damage. However, when we allow our imagination to be used by God as part of a holy adventure, it can show us amazing and wonderful things. Do not be afraid to give your imagination to God during your prayer and study. Allow Him to show you things. But always be mindful to test the spirit and know it is God's voice you are hearing. 1 John 4 gives us a roadmap for how to do this, and I will have more on that later.

I journal as part of my time with God. Journaling is a way for me to dump everything out of my brain in order to make space. Journaling helps ground me and allows me to stop toiling over issues. For me, it is better than dumping my mess onto others. It allows me to let it go, give it to God, and pray it through. About four years ago, as I prayed and studied, God laid out the plan for what I thought would become this book. It was not a laborious effort, but a strike from Heaven into my spirit. In the blink of an eye, the strike was there, like, *here it is, now get it done.*

In a matter of minutes, God gave me the title and the chapter outline that I penned into my leather journal and began to pray over. Since then, writing the rest has gone much slower. This isn't because God's direction was any less clear, but because I got in His way and in my own way. Perhaps you know the feeling? Maybe you too *know* God has shown you something and your obedience has been slow.

After I wrote the outline down in my journal and prayed over it that day, I ran, hid, circled slowly, and talked about doing it, but was afraid to actually do what God had shown me. Fear of failure will get us every single time, girls. If we think it is about what we have to offer instead of what He has to offer through us, we will fail. It is not about you or about me. It is about He who is in us. He holds the power and the purpose of our days. I have asked for His forgiveness. And God, because He is the God of second chances, gave me another opportunity to write a book for Him.

However, as I began to write, He changed my direction back to words and ideas He had given me some twenty years ago—not the ones in my journal. I started with one concept; He morphed and changed my direction and scope, pulling in pieces and ideas from long ago and adding them to recent lessons I had written for our women's study group at my church. Why do I think this happened? I knew it was because a global pandemic hit, and chaos abounded in America. Perspectives have changed and when that happened, needs changed, and new or different messages must be both shared and heard.

God places strategic moments in our lives to remind us that He has crafted and chosen us. If we allow Him, He assumes control. Make no mistake, it is a choice. You have free will to accept God and Christ as His divine Son, or to reject them. He will not force you to believe or follow Him. You are not His slave.

He will pursue the lost and try to win their hearts, but God will never make anyone choose to serve Him. If God made people serve, then, by definition, they would become His slaves. That is not how the Kingdom of God operates. We are His children, and He is the Father. He is not a cosmic bully, a genie in the sky, or a slaveholder. God is the giver of every good gift,[2] and in tragedy, He is an anchor for broken vessels.

I want you to be fully aware that part of this book is about *amazing* women found in scripture, but they are not all "main characters". They may only have one or two verses written about them in the Bible which I believe to be the infallible Word of God. As we discover their contexts and encounters, I am asking you to put yourself into the stories of these women. What might we feel? What might we see? What might we hear or smell? How can what we know of them from scripture, other scholarly historical accounts such as the works of Josephus, and Jewish documentation help us imagine their journey more vividly? How can we stretch what we know and see to apply these lessons to our own lives?

Let me explain through an example: Have you ever imagined being David, standing in the middle of the battlefield facing Goliath? Here you are, a boy who is miniature compared to the G-I-A-N-T in front of you. You know your brothers are fuming mad at you for agreeing to fight when they and their army buddies would not. The king himself gave you his armor so you would have some kind of protection, but you cannot wear it. It makes you feel 100 pounds heavier and you cannot move freely. It was not made for you, so you throw it to the ground and fully commit to the God of Israel as your Protector.

Can you feel the slingshot in your palm, with its smooth handle, worn from use while protecting the flocks? It is your favorite one because it has just the right balance when pulled. Can you imagine the kinds of rocks you gathered? They had to be just the right size and shape for maximum speed, velocity, and injury. They are not just rocks, but your skillfully chosen weapons.

Can you envision the hot Israeli desert sun beating down upon your face? You look up and throw your arm above your eyes so you can see more clearly under its shade. You will have to be mindful of the sun and its shadows when the fight begins. Can you dream of how fast your heart would be beating? You run recklessly onto the battlefield, sling shot drawn with your best rock in it, and scream for God to show up and show off. The only other alternative is your own demise!

Then, it happens. You launch the stone and the battle is on. It hits! He staggers and falls dead!! Can you conceive the noise of his body landing with full force upon the ground? Can you feel the vibrations of the earth as his massive weight crashes in the dust? Can you hear the shouts and maneuvers of the armies, the sound of your own voice, the cry of your prayer, the thumping of your heart and your feet? You are still alive! The enemy has been vanquished! Praise God for delivering Israel from her enemies, PRAISE GOD!

This is part of what we will be doing with our imaginations and the stories of women in scripture. I will also share with you part of my personal life story. I make no pretense to be perfect. On any given day, I may be a hot mess in need of an extraordinary rescue. It's not easy for me to be vulnerable and allow my imagination or my story be available to you. I have read, researched, prayed, written, rewritten, and rewritten some more. My prayer is that the stories and words written here strike your heart and guide you to your own victory against your giants.

The challenge I give to you is this: *Can you set aside what you have always known about women in the Bible to take a new look at their stories from a different perspective? Are you secure enough to investigate what you can learn that might alter your vision or have bearing upon your heart or mind?*

In every way, I implore you to take what you read back to scripture and find God's truths around the topics and themes. His Word is perfect. I also encourage you to dig deeper with new references, Biblical historians, rabbinical and theological teachings, and into your own personal faith journey.

For me, I have chosen Whom I serve. One of His names is Jesus Christ, Yeshua in Hebrew. I have many friends from different faiths, and my hope is that they are never offended but always curious about why I choose Jesus. I am just a girl trying to get my Jesus story right. Thankfully, He is not done with me yet. Each time I read scripture, I keep an eye out for new lessons.

My hope is that you gain a new perspective on the stories of these women from scripture who were imperfect, broken, used, and redeemed. Girls, they were just like us in so many ways. They were not infallible or perfect, but God chose to let their stories be told. They are in His holy scriptures for a reason.

Imagine, if you can, your life's highlight reel, your social media feed, and your life's "B-roll" being viewed. The footage from mountaintop successes and the raw unused parts—the trashy pieces you do not want anyone to see—equally plastered for everyone to examine throughout eternity. What would it show? How would it read? Unfortunately, for me, it would depend upon the time in my life when it was captured. It may be the same for you, but God redeems it all.

He gives grace. He calls us. He waits and He perseveres. God called me to write so long ago. Each time I tried, I chickened out after a few steps forward. I made progress but never completed it until now. I am thankful and blessed by the fact God kept giving me more chances and relentlessly pursued me. He is not done with me yet, nor is He done with you.

REAL WOMEN FROM SCRIPTURE: ZIPPORAH

We were simply doing what was asked of us and what was necessary. We needed to water our flocks. In this dry, sun-soaked land, water is essential for survival. As we approached the well, many angry men surrounded us. They were demanding we back off and let them have first rank with their flocks. Suddenly, this foreigner stood strong and defended us. Why would he do this? We did not know of his upbringing, but we knew he did not look like us.

My name is Zipporah and I am of Arabic descent; a Midianite to be exact. My family and I come from the land of the East around the Gulf of Arabia and Mount Sinai. This man looked Egyptian. He was dark, well-skilled, regal in some ways. He stood up for the injustice he witnessed. My sisters and I were grateful for his help and quickly completed our task with his assistance. There was definitely something unusual about this man. He exhibited such uncommon behaviors. Men do not usually serve women nor do men of his class serve animals as common practice. Nonetheless, we appreciated all he did for us.

My sisters and I rushed home to speak with our father as soon as we finished watering the animals. I am the oldest of seven and thankful I could tell my father the story with a favorable ending. I do not know what would have happened had the stranger not been there when trouble arose. We recanted what transpired. Our father asked why we had left this traveler at the well. He was a foreigner and likely needed a place to stay.

Sometimes, as a woman, it is challenging to know what is right. Our father, Jethro, also called Reul by some, was a Midianite priest. We have customs and rules for women, as do all other lands around us. As a woman, if we speak to a man before he speaks to us, or just because we want to, we will have broken the laws and customs of our land. How was I to know my father would question us about where the man was? How could I have possibly imagined Father would want us to bring a strange man to our home?

Nonetheless, at Father's direction, we hurried back to the well and found the stranger. Tired, but relieved he was still there, I extended the invitation to come break bread with us. As we walked with him back to our home, I had no idea how one dinner invitation from my father would change my life. From that day forward, this man called Moses lived with our family. He helped keep our flocks and tended them for many years.

In due time, my father gave him my hand in marriage. One act of kindness on his part, and one dinner invitation on Father's part, led to my wedding and the eventual birth of two sons, Gershom and Eliezer. I wish this story could end here without regret and with a nice joy-filled finish, but marriage does not always work out easily. I had a duty and I wanted to see it through. There was just one problem: faith.

My husband's faith journey was not mine.[3] I was the eldest daughter of a Midianite priest, so I understood worship and God, to some extent. Our people came from Abraham's line through his second wife after Sarah: Keturah. Abraham and Keturah had six sons, and Midian, our forefather, was one of them. However, I did not understand this special calling God had on my husband and I did not agree with all the laws of his faith. I did not always understand why he did things as he did. It was alien to me.

Over the years, I found out he was Hebrew by bloodline. However, he had been plucked out of a river in a basket as a baby and brought up by the daughter of Egypt's pharaoh. He appeared Egyptian and knew their customs because he grew up in their palace. There were a great deal of details surrounding his birth and upbringing that I could not fully perceive. When I had first met him, Moses had fled from Egypt for killing a man who harmed a Hebrew slave. That is why he was in Midian.

There were days when I just could not fathom his spiritual quests. Then there was the inner drive I would see come over him which was unexplainable at times. It seemed like his God actually spoke to him. It frightened me in some ways. I tried to be a good wife. I tried to love him and allow him to love me, but he was walking such a different journey than me. Many times, it seemed like a road divided. We were walking together but separately at the same time.

One day Moses came home from tending the flocks on the back side of the desert. He told an alarming story of how God had appeared to him in a burning bush. He said God had commanded him to return to Egypt. He was supposed to deliver a message from God and demand Pharaoh let the Israelites go. My mind could not reason it out. How could this be true?

My husband was to be a spokesman in Egypt to help free His people. My husband, who could not always speak well and was better with his hands than his words, was going to be a spokesman? Apparently, he did not understand it all either. He explained to my Father that he had begged God to send someone else. During this encounter, he told of how God had shown mercy to him.

Aaron, Moses' brother, will be allowed to go on the journey and speak for Moses, however, Moses will have signs from God to show the people. What does this mean? We will undoubtedly be in danger. What mother wants her sons to be placed directly into the path of oncoming danger? Am I supposed to let their father's own hands lead us into slaughter? It sounds insane and I feel very unsettled about it all.

Nonetheless, I try to be obedient to my husband and my father. I try to do what is right and what is expected, even as I swallow the lump in my throat. I wrap my sons in protective clothing, gather our things, and set out on this journey with Moses from my land of Midian to Egypt. Where are we going? What will happen to us?

We were on the way to my husband's assignment from God. He was apparently destined to do wonders in Egypt.

I was uncomfortable, frightened, and unsure of what to expect. But Moses was driven by a purpose bigger than himself. There was no talking him out of this journey, even though I had once managed to convince him not to circumcise our son. In my mind, it was a dangerous and unnecessary practice. None of my people did this and the men functioned fine. There was no need for what I considered a barbaric custom, in my faith or in my heart as a mother.

Sometime into our journey, we were attacked by hardship and sickness. My husband fell ill and was near death. Hadn't we started this journey under God's direction? Were we not doing what was required? Why was God allowing Moses to suffer? What was happening? I was incredibly frustrated and kept replaying these events in my mind.

Circumcision! Moses had told me of God's command to circumcise our son. Yet I begged him to do no harm or touch our boy in this way. I could not imagine the need for this pain being inflicted upon baby boys. That night, I realized how big the God of the Israelites was. In anger or panic, maybe in a vain attempt to appease this force from above, I took the knife into my own hands and cut my child's foreskin off. I will never forget that piercing scream from my baby. You may know the sound.

Tears.

There was so much blood. Stop! Make it all end.

> *"Then Zipporah took a flint and cut off her son's foreskin*
> *and touched Moses' feet with it and said,*
> *'Surely you are a bridegroom of blood to me!'"*
> (Exodus 4:25)

My words were not pretty. My hands were not pretty. My heart? It changed that night. I am grateful Moses was saved; his life spared. No matter my words, the attack on his life stopped, but we stopped too. I was done.[4] My son survived and grew up. But things were never the same between Moses and me again. This journey was not mine. I did not choose it and I did not want it.

Moses went on into Egypt, freed his people and did many great things in the eyes of the Israelites and their God. But who am I? The wife of a mighty man of the God of Israel, but I am not an Israelite and soon we were estranged. I wished Moses no harm and he wished me none either. However, I went back to Midian and took my boys with me. Perhaps it was partly my decision, or my father's, or perhaps it was all Moses' idea. I do not remember, and it did not matter; I just wanted to get away from him.

After some time, my father took us all to visit Moses. He talked with Moses and gave him some sound advice about how to rule and give judgments. Moses listened and followed his advice.

During the entire visit, my husband and I never spoke. Silence can be loud and brash in a marriage. Even though we did not speak, perhaps he prayed God was not done with me yet. I would never know. We remained silent.

Girls, perhaps you have distance and silence in your marriage just as Zipporah had with Moses. Perhaps you have made a choice to not believe, or not believe yet. Perhaps you and your husband do not share the same faith. There are lessons to be learned in the seeking and in the quiet. While Zipporah is mentioned again in scripture and considered a central figure in the Jewish faith, she is never mentioned being beside Moses again outside of these verses in the Bible.

For more scriptures on Zipporah, see Exodus 2:18-24, 4:18-26, and 18:1-6.

REAL BATTLES: Faith, Do You Believe?

One of the choices we get to make during this lifetime is to believe in God or reject Him. He will pursue the lost, but He will never demand we give up our ability to choose Him and submit. There have been long standing arguments against this fact, even within the Christian community. If we believe God chooses only certain children, then we must also believe in the converse: that He rejects and has intentionally appointed others for damnation.

If you are not sure about God yet, then I encourage you to continue reading from the perspective of what you can learn for further self-insight. I also invite you to develop a better understanding of why, by the world's standards, a highly educated woman such as myself would choose to become a follower of Christ. Faith is not dead, and religion is not what some make it appear to be, so take the journey for yourself.

My prayer for you, is that somewhere within these pages, there is enough evidence to point you to the truth of a supreme Creator. Question, search, and look at it from every angle. You are not an accident from your parents or through evolution. Evolution could not make our intricate bodies work. There must be a Creator. Examine the life of Christ and His works. Chase the truth.

If you are a fan of God and believe Jesus is His divine Son, or you are a fan of God, but you are not sure about the divinity of Christ, continue reading. I pray you learn and grow new roots through your study of the lessons within this book. However, I also pray you are more than an admirer. Admiration does not always make one commit to buying the object of their adoration.

If you are a devoted Christian who follows the teaching of Christ and aims to become more like His example, I pray you have strength and perseverance for your journey. I pray you receive a fresh perspective on the stories in the pages that follow even if you have heard them before. I also long for you to read the stories about women you may have never really noticed before. God has left nothing to chance. Each man, woman, and situation in His Word are there for a reason.

Whether you believe yet or not, whether you follow yet or not, whether you know all these stories or not are all moot points. What is important is your faith and your willingness to remain open-minded as you explore the content that follows. Your ability to set aside preconceptions or misconceptions will help you do the work of reading and reflecting. You will most likely find parts of your story here or stories similar to your own. Each time you do, reflect on what you might be learning from them. Ultimately, what you will gain and to what extent you do so, are your choice.

Developing faith and new insight are like growing seeds. When a seed is planted, it takes time to mature. You need patience and a good bit of study beforehand as you go through the process. Nurture what begins to grow. Little-by-little, it will take root, sprout, blossom and mature.

REAL POWER FOR THE REAL WORLD: Your Birthright

Maybe you are at a crossroads in your faith quest, or in the middle of a crisis of faith. You may have come to the moment when you must decide if you want to keep searching, believe in God, or follow Him more intimately. It happens. The question is, what will you do with it? What will you inherit?

Connecting the head and the heart is not always easy. Medically speaking, I have heard it said many times, there is an eighteen-inch distance, on average, between the brain and the heart. Eighteen inches can seem like a chasm the size of a canyon. One of the first steps in bridging this gap is to unwrap the truth of God's character.

God cannot lie because He cannot be anything other than who He is, so part of your assignment here is to study His characteristics. Satan can and does lie all the time because it is who he is, so study him, too. I urge you not to study God's character to win an argument or prove your point for a particular situation. Instead, study God with your whole heart and mind. When those two things align, your beliefs strengthen, and you can better recognize the enemy's lies.

Satan is a liar whose purpose is to steal from you. It is his core. When you know you have a birthright through Jesus Christ, you make it harder for Satan to take it away. Girl, you were created for a purpose, but you must be willing to become part of God's family. Satan will tell you all kinds of lies that appear as truth. He is the master deceiver, and his sole purpose is to destroy your birthright and God given mission. But accepting Christ as the true Lord (ruler) of your life guarantees you a place in Heaven and the right to claim your God given inheritance for eternity. Don't walk away from Him.

Get Real: Reflection & Prayer

1. What stood out to you from Zipporah's story?

2. What was a new idea for you?

3. What parts of your own story do you need to share so others can learn from it?

4. If you could be totally honest with yourself in your faith journey, what score would you give yourself? Zero being "I do not believe" and five being "I am ready to develop the deepest roots of my life thus far." Why did you pick that score?

5. What two things do you want to work towards after studying this chapter?

6. What is one truth you know about God?

7. What is one thing you want to explore about Him?

Father God,

Help me to take a step closer towards You today. I pray my eyes will be opened, my ears will hear only You, and my mind will focus. Give me what I need to take the next step forward in my journey with You. I accept the gift of salvation promised in Ephesians 2:8. Help me to have grace with myself and others. Most of all, show me mercy as I grow.

I pray in Jesus' name,

Amen.

CHAPTER 2

Girl Tribe

"And He awoke and rebuked the wind and said to the sea, 'Peace! Be still!" And the wind ceased, and there was a great calm."
(Mark 4:39)

REAL LIFE: Things Change

Most Americans would not deny that 2020 did not meet their expectations; at least, as they dreamed and made resolutions on New Year's Eve 2019. I am fairly confident no one hoisted a glass at midnight and toasted to a global pandemic, murder hornets, toilet paper shortages, civil unrest, senseless murder of people because of their skin tones, disbanding of police, coin shortages, record setting floods and snowstorms, and more ridiculous fighting within our government offices or on our capital grounds. I am in no way belittling these events. Their reality is simply unfathomable. Surely no one imagined all this as they made their plans for a new year.

As hard as it was, that's life sometimes, right? We often have dreams, ideas, and visions of how things will go that never play out the way we thought. Sometimes they work out better than we hoped and sometimes worse. But rarely do we experience exactly what we map out. When we do, somehow, we seem surprised and say things like, "That went according to plan." We celebrate the success.

In the mid 2000's, I had visions of big things. I had just completed my doctoral work and began looking into new job opportunities. My husband, Daryl, was an incredibly supportive encourager for me. He was a champion by my side every single day. I would often joke about being his show-and-tell object because he talked about me to *everyone*. He was so proud of me and the nature of who he was made me want to become a better human being.

Then, on January 9, 2012, I came home from work and found him on the floor of his home office. In the seconds it took me to get across the room to him, I vividly remember saying in my mind, "This is where everything changes." My body moved quickly but my mind was in slow motion, like a video at half-speed. Suddenly, all of my plans—a new career for me, travel for us, checking off our bucket list items together—came to a screeching halt. All that mattered was saving this man who had loved me so well for so long. A life and death battle literally played out before my eyes.

For nine and a half weeks, we warred for Daryl. Our amazing network of supportive friends and family would sit with him at the hospital so I could take a two-hour break from the Intensive Care Unit. When he was released to rehab, they would "coach" him in physical therapy, cheer him on and offer encouragement so I could go to work because I was out of paid leave.

After eight weeks, we were released to in-home therapy and rehab. Our friends brought us meals, made ramps in our home for his wheelchair, ran errands, and prayed. Oh, how they prayed! We were told of churches in various towns that stopped services and petitioned God on Daryl's behalf at critical moments. He was that kind of man…so loved and respected. They were those kinds of friends. They were deep in the trenches of our battlefield trying to take back territory the enemy wanted to steal.

He had been home for about a week when tragedy struck. He died in my arms in our bedroom. On March 16, 2012, Daryl got his true going-home date. He went to heaven and I was left here on earth with the biggest battle I had ever faced. My dreams were shattered, and my life strewn in a million tiny pieces all over a hardwood floor.

Make no mistake, Girls. We are all at war in some way and the battles are real. But, God's Word says, *"and they conquered him by the blood of the lamb and the word of their testimonies…"*.(Revelation 12:11a)

Our stories matter. Our testimony is the story of how God has met and changed us; how we have seen evidence of His work in our lives.

Your story matters just as much as mine. If it helps someone get real with themselves, those they love, or with God, isn't your story worth telling? My story is not always pretty. Yet I promise you I am blessed. I am blessed, not because I am amazing, or cool, or worthy, but because God is all those and so much more. And He can use my greatest tragedies for His highest glory if I allow the stories to be told.

In my life, He has gathered my shattered pieces and reformed them into something useful hundreds of times just like He has done in the lives of so many women throughout history. He is the greatest Healer of all time.

REAL WOMEN FROM SCRIPTURE: THE GIRL TRIBE

Life in the desert was not always easy. A life constantly on the move wasn't always fun. Travel and adventure can sometimes be hard work. But, when you have a group of like-minded people to journey and work with and when you know your mission could someday save the world, you do what needs to be done, even if your efforts will go unrecognized.

> *"Soon afterward he went on through cities and villages, proclaiming and bringing the good news of the kingdom of God. And the twelve were with him, and also some women who had been healed of evil spirits and infirmities: Mary, called Magdalene, from whom seven demons had gone out, and Joanna, the wife of Chuza, Herod's household manager, and Susanna, and many others, who provided for them out of their means."*
> (Luke 8:1-3)

There we are, do you see us? We are a fierce tribe of women. Most of us have been outcasts in need of healing, servants of the king in need of saving, and once bound but now free.

Each of our individual stories are unique. Some are more shocking, scandalous, and harsh than yours. Some are less so, but each one of us has been touched and profoundly changed by a man named Jesus. You will know when the fingertip of Christ touches you, just as we did. How? He leaves an imprint that will forever change the trajectory of your life's story.

His impression upon our hearts has moved us. The question is, will you allow His impression upon your heart to so greatly impact you that you are willing to follow Him, no matter what you have to walk away from, or where He leads?

We gave Him all we had. Our money, time, and talents were used to make Him better known. We took care of Jesus and His disciples — those He intimately taught as they followed Him daily. We journeyed with Christ and the disciples to share The Good News that He was the Messiah. We chose to be servants as a girl tribe. We were tasked with cooking, cleaning, finding shelter, and making provisions for Jesus and His inner circle. Many times, we used our own funds to provide for our needs as we traveled together. We shared what we had with all those around us so that everyone had a fair portion.

Many could not understand that we served and gave not because we were enslaved, but because we were free. Christ had set us free! We had been freed from evil spirits, sickness, infirmities, and false gods. Our friend, Mary Magdalene, was freed from seven demons. Her healing was real, and she was a new woman. We all had stories from our past lives, but as we traveled together and learned the truths of Jesus, those stories became part of our healing and hope.

Girls, can you fathom the kind of freedom that led each of these women to walk away from everything they had known, and make a choice to say, "I am all in"?

Could you imagine being so focused on serving your tribe of like-minded believers that you would risk bodily harm, imprisonment, or capture? Can you imagine what it would have been like to walk so closely with Christ and to be near Him as a compassionate caretaker?

These women served by choice. They gave by choice. They left their homes to become servant followers by choice. They loved full out and all in, by choice. That is true freedom. Freedom to go and freedom to stay. Where are you today — enslaved or serving? What is your choice?

If you would like to read more scriptures on the more obscure women mentioned here, see Matthew 27:55-56, Luke 23:55-24:10.

REAL BATTLES: Naysayers

There will always be dream killers and naysayers, people telling us we cannot do something. They may not even know us or our capabilities. Tragically they may be part of our family or among our friends. The enemy is forever on the prowl to kill, steal, and destroy (John 10:10). Modern day Sadducees do exist. They are people of wealth and elite stature holding to a strict interpretation of the law. They look down on those who do not conform to the law, word for word. They practice the religious rituals without a heart bathed in faithful relationship.

Modern day Pharisees are still around, too; people of moderate means holding to a more flexible interpretation of the law. They are called hypocrites - speaking the law but not living it. I have been this person in the past. I knew what was right, told people what was right, and at the same time I was not living it out. I have coveted and wanted to appear more than I actually am. I was an example of a modern-day Pharisee.

The battle that still exists between these two groups is no less real today than in the time of Christ. They tear each other down and try to persuade us to conform. Meanwhile, we are caught in the middle or pressed to choose sides. The only side I want to choose is Jesus.

Even if we live the most charmed and blessed lives, eventually we will face a giant who tries to break us down or make us live with their point of view. So, what do we do when it happens? Turn to Jesus, read the truth from the Bible, know why it is the truth, and be part of the only tribe that matters for eternity. If this is not something you are sure how to do or believe yet, that is okay. Keep reading. There is no condemnation in Christ. Seek, question, and remain open to your learning journey.

REAL POWER FOR THE REAL WORLD: God Tribes

After the chaos of finding my husband on the floor, calling paramedics, transporting him to the ER and having so many people meet us there, I was lost for words. Over the next nine hours, I just kept repeating to myself and those gathered around me, "His grace is sufficient." A dear friend came through the front door of the ER in tears. As I hugged him and cried, it was all I could say over and over. I held onto that scripture until Daryl was moved to ICU during the wee hours of the morning.

"His grace is sufficient" comes from a verse in 2 Corinthians 12, where Paul is talking about his weakness and how, in his suffering, he had to become totally dependent upon Christ's power. It was hidden in my heart and they were the only words I could squeeze out of my trauma filled mind.

Around 2:00 a.m., I stepped out of ICU into a packed waiting room right outside the oversized wooden doors. When they opened, the cold air rushed out from behind me. As the doors closed, the clanging of the metal was harsh and loud. Every chair in that area was full of people who loved my husband, Daryl. Eyes filled with tears and faces full of pain and concern stared back at me.

As I looked around, I noticed there were six pastors from five different churches among our friends who had gathered. I spoke for a moment about being a childless couple who often wonders what their legacy will be, but that in this moment I knew these people and their churches were part of Daryl's legacy. Many of those people were the tribe who carried me through the coming weeks and years.

In those moments, I fully understood why we are supposed to have a church family. More than ever, I understood why we are commanded to memorize scripture. We need both a church family and God's Word buried within when life shatters. His people and His Scripture came forward when we needed them most.

His Word did not return void; it helped soothe my soul and put my emotions in check under God's authority. Though I spoke this scripture and I knew it, there would be days that followed when I would question it.

Was God's grace sufficient for all we were facing?

Was this what abundant life looked like?

Would Daryl and I both make it through this?

Could I go on if he did not?

God was big enough to handle my questions and He can manage yours too. Don't think your questions are so big and so hard that God cannot supply all the answers you seek. Make a choice to ask the hard questions.

Get Real: Reflection & Prayer

1. Where are you today? Are you enslaved or free? If you are enslaved to something name it and begin to pray for your handcuffs and shackles to be removed.

2. Have you seen evidence of His fingerprint on your life or are you desperately searching for evidence that He is real?

3. Are you listening to naysayers in your life? What are their whispers and what is God's truth?

4. Would you have followed even if you have had to give up everything or everyone? Be truthful with yourself. Keep it real.

5. Explain a time in your life when you may have questioned God. If you could ask God a few questions, what might you want to discuss or know?

6. Who needs to become part of your tribe? Why are they important for you?

7. What do you sometimes struggle with in your own life, but point out in others' lives? What can you do about this?

Father God,

Help me to lean into You more than I lean into others when my world breaks and I face giants. Give me strength, wisdom, and perseverance. Help me to memorize Your Word and bring it to my heart and mind when I need it most.

In Jesus' name I pray,

Amen.

CHAPTER 3

When Life Stops, Where Do We Fall?

"For God alone, O my soul, wait in silence, for my hope is from him."
(Psalm 62:5)

REAL LIFE: Halted

The world ground to a halt and stopped us in our tracks early in the pandemic. For the first time, many of us were made to stand still and take time off. However, maybe we did not stand still in His presence. Maybe it was all too chaotic and too much at once for us to dwell on God. Being still is not always easy or restful. For some, it was hard to find peace and quiet while they tried to figure out how to work from home. Others had to make sure kids did their schoolwork because they suddenly became a homeschool parent. For many, it was hard to run a household with everyone home for long extended periods of time.

The frustration, pressure, and sorrow of figuring out a new normal may have pushed stillness to the side, urgent prayer to the top, and life into a different kind of overdrive. If this was the case, be aware of what you lost. Did you lose security, status, time, or control? Did you become angry or frightened?

Sometimes we do not recognize that what we feel is grief. Grief is a companion of loss. It is a normal reaction to the imbalance of what we are missing.

Even when we survive a great loss or life brings us to a halt, being still is a choice. For some of us, it is neither easy nor comfortable. If I have learned anything during this life journey, it is that God does not care if I am comfortable. He cares if I am obedient. Being still with Him, spending time reading the Bible, praying, worshipping, fasting — these are things He commands us to do. At the end of the day, though, they are still choices we have to make. Imagine how much He wants us to make the choices that lead us closer to Him. He does not command us to control us, He commands us because He knows what is best for us.

So, what if we learned to sit and soak in the Word of God just as Mary sat at the feet of Jesus instead of running around the house like her sister, Martha, busying herself during His visit? (Luke 10:38-42) Instead, Mary soaked in the words from His lips like a soft sponge gulps up a single drop of water. Is this what would give us peace in the middle of chaos? Would it give us balance in midst of imbalance?

REAL WOMEN FROM SCRIPTURE: MARY OF BETHANY

I heard their whispers and murmurs. I knew they were not happy with me being here. I am Mary of Bethany and I did not choose serving over sitting, racing over reflection, or my agenda and expectations over His essence. I chose to be still. I chose to be quiet. I chose His companionship, His instruction, His presence. I chose to see and believe.

Trust me when I tell you, I knew I was out of place. No one had to point it out to me. By the world's standard and our cultural rules, I did not "belong" in the room with the Rabbi. They talked about me behind my back and sometimes in front of me, but their word jabs did not change my place. I sat. I listened and thought things through. I learned and my faith deepened with each word spoken by Jesus of Nazareth.

I was so captivated and enamored by Jesus and His words that most of the time, I did not even notice anyone else was around. All my spirit and ears wanted to hear was the sound of His voice and the depth of His teaching. I was always listening for Him instead of to them. What would He say next? How would His eyes narrow or His inflection and cadence change as He taught lessons and told stories?

Jesus gave me a place. To my countrymen it was not a place of honor, but to me it was everything. To them, only lowly servants sat at someone's feet. Servants washed the dirt, mud, and muck off the feet of the wealthy or stationed. Those who were worthy of cleanliness and a place at the table were served, not servants. To be at someone's feet was the last place anyone wanted to be...anyone except me.

By nature, I am quiet and reflective. I think more than I speak, and my emotions are much more central to me than the business and affairs of daily life. My sister Martha gets frustrated with me about this sometimes. She is always so hurried and focused on working and serving. I understand her desire to serve and the duty she feels towards it, but I do not think she always understands my choices nor my sensitivity.

When Jesus and His followers come here to our home, she runs about preparing and cleaning. She becomes stressed because she wants everything perfect for them and our brother Lazarus. On the other hand, I focus on how I can position myself in the room to get closer to listen. I want to be able to hear and gaze up at Jesus because it helps me remember His lessons.

My spirit and mind are captivated by His wisdom and kindness. I know it is against our customs and rules for a woman to be seen sitting in the company of men to hear the same teaching. Yet, I am bold and brave, even in my silence, because their feelings and desires do not matter as much as His words and what I gain from them.

One day, when Jesus visited our home, I positioned myself exactly where I wanted to be: at His feet. I had pursued this place left vacant by others. I was so close; I could see His eyes and His expressions. I could hear the strength and authority in His voice.

As I listened carefully, I could hear His breath as he drew air in for his next sentence. In that place, nothing else in the world mattered to me, except Him.

One…

    Single…

        Intense…

            Intimate…

                Focus…

                    Jesus.

His words rang loudly with God's truths. When they settled into my heart, I knew their power. I wish there had been more days like this, but Jesus came and went from our town as He traveled. We knew He loved our home and He loved us. But then, the unthinkable happened.

My brother became extremely sick. We sent word for Jesus to come because we believed He could not only help but He would heal Lazarus. But He had not come quickly enough, and Lazarus died. I became desperately sad and even disappointed. If He loved us so much, why had He not rushed to us? There were no answers in the silence of that day. We cried and prepared my brother's body for burial.

Where was He?

After four days, Jesus of Nazareth finally arrived in Bethany. We could not have known that Jesus was about to use us to display the glory of God. My sister and I were both so grief-stricken, but she ran to meet Him as soon as we heard of His coming. I could not get up.[5] It was too much; my heart was too heavy.

Soon, Martha came back to frantically encourage me to go with her. She said Jesus was asking for me where she had met Him on the roadside. Something in my spirit leapt. I jumped up and began to run with many mourners following behind me. We had no idea how our lives would change that day.

My heart was pounding and my body ached. When I saw Him, I fell at His feet and wept. I was overcome by my emotions and could not hold my tears in any longer. I cried and spoke the truth; "Lord, if You had been here, my brother would not have died."[6] In that instant, Jesus wept with us. Our sorrow became His sorrow, but only for a moment. In the next few minutes, He called out to Lazarus and brought him back to life. I could not believe what I saw. My brother soon came out of the grave, half-wrapped in his burial garments but very much alive.

JESUS!

One single focus…Jesus. He had brought the dead back to life and those of us who watched were forever changed. My love for Him and devotion to Him would never again waver, not even for a second.

As the time of His earthly death neared, I could not stop. I had to do it. There was nothing that could have stopped me. Judas was furious and condemned my actions, but just like before, I did not listen to his words nor did I care what his opinion was. I did what my spirit prompted me to do.

Jesus had brought my brother back to life and I was convinced He was the Messiah. He was the one our faith foretold. My spirit was compelled to anoint his feet with my most expensive perfume. I cannot explain it. At times, I surprised even myself. This was one of those nights, but deep down, I understood the teaching and I knew He was about to be taken from us.

There was a celebration feast being held at Simon's house. Simon had once been an outcast leper.[7] That night was a testament to the real power of Jesus Christ. In the home of a healed leper, we celebrated a dead man walking out of his burial garments alive. It is almost impossible to imagine the excitement and festivities, yet there was an undertone in the mood. We knew this was big. Jesus was big; bigger than anything the world had ever known.

Martha was busy serving as I stared at my alabaster box. It was so beautiful and the contents inside it were precious. Some would have had to work for a year, or more, to be able to purchase such a rare perfume. I was not naive to its value, but Jesus was much more valuable to me than anything I owned. My spirit was pressed to do this as a way of saying thank you, preparing Him, and honoring Him.

I simply had to take my place, at his feet.

Once I was there, I opened the box and poured out its contents. All eyes were fixed upon me as I took down my hair, its length and beauty on display. The smells and aromas of the perfume were strong and exquisite, my hair long and flowing. I wiped his feet dry as I leaned in ever so close and allowed my hair to soak in the oils and His power. The room was stunned because I had gone against many of our teachings and rules. Yet, my spirit was full.

I cannot explain to you how this felt. I was surrounded by a party that had grown silent, and there I was on the floor, right where I felt the most comfortable. The silence was broken by Judas bellowing about the cost and why this treasure had been wasted instead of sold. He droned on about the money which should have been added to the purse so it could have been given to the poor. We would later find out that he was angry because he was a thief and a liar. Had I sold it and given the money to him for the ministry, Judas would have stolen some of it.

The power of Jesus' voice pierced through his hollow words and quieted Judas. Witnessing that action, the others knew it was not a time to speak. So, there we were, Jesus' feet anointed, my spirit full, and others left wondering what to do next. Soon, He would be gone.

On His darkest day at the cross, I prayed my Lord remembered that night and the perfume from my alabaster box. Only then did I fully understand why I had been so pressed to anoint His feet. It was as if I were preparing Him in a small way for the day they crucified Him.

I am Mary of Bethany and I was honored to listen, watch, pursue, and be still at the feet of Jesus. He knew me even when I did not utter a sound, just like He knows you in your innermost being.[8]

Girls, Jesus knew her thoughts, her longings, her misgivings, and shortcomings more than she knew them herself. He also loved her, and He longs to love us this intimately too. So today, I remind myself, "Shut your mouth, woman of God. There is a better way."

Choose to sit with Jesus. Be still…listen. He has a mission for each of His children that no one else was created to do.

For more reading on this complex woman, Mary of Bethany, read Mark 14:3-11, Luke 10: 38-42, and John 11-12.

REAL BATTLES: My Tongue Problem

Early in my life, I had to apologize a lot for losing control of my mouth more often than I care to tell. My tongue is quick and sharp and caused many bleeding gashes and deep wounds to myself and those around me. If I became angry or defensive, I would say hurtful things to push people away. The enemy knew just how to pressure me so my mouth would spout out without thought or prayer. I needed a heart change so I could have a mouth change. What comes out of the mouth is a sign of the heart.

> *"But what comes out of the mouth proceeds from the heart, and this defiles a person."*
> (Matthew 15:18)

In a very practical way, I have had to learn not to say the first three things that come to mind. Most days, I make it to about thought ten before I let something come out of my mouth during a difficult conversation. I must measure my words with purpose. Is what I am about to say important? Is it beneficial to all concerned? Is it chosen or impulsive? Does it cause harm or good?

These are the kinds of questions we should ask ourselves. Leaving a tempting sentence unsaid can save embarrassment, apologies, and hurt feelings.

I love this quote by British author Dorothy Neville-Rolfe, "The real art of conversation is not only to say the right thing at the right place, but to leave unsaid the wrong thing at the most tempting moment."[9] I believe it to be one of the most difficult adaptations for my tongue. However, it is also crucial for my work and the health of my relationships.

Perhaps you have a tongue problem, too. What you think is funny, others may not. Maybe what you say is often misinterpreted. Perhaps it is body language, tone, or word choice. No matter the cause of strife, the mouth can offer a problem or a solution.

REAL POWER FOR THE REAL WORLD:
Measure Words and Love Extravagantly

Just as Christ met Mary in the middle of the road, He longs to meet us right where we are and encourage us to move forward. Just as she measured words carefully, the weight of what we choose to say and what we leave unsaid should be ever present in our thoughts and conversations. Mary sat and listened much more than she ran and spoke. There was wisdom in her actions. Can you imagine how many times she might have wanted to speak? How many times might she have had to bite her tongue, or determine that her words would not add enough value?

Our words matter. When we fail to choose carefully, we can leave wounded people in our wake. If we storm into a situation with our mouth first, instead of our mind or our spirit, we can damage relationships we have worked years to develop.

Words cannot be unspoken. Our families, companies, and churches can be broken apart within minutes. There was an old rhyme, "Sticks and stones may break my bones, but words can never hurt me." It is a lie, but it was made up so we could try to learn the principle of not letting words cut us to our core. The emotional and psychological wounds that damaging words leave behind are real and we must heal from them in order to move forward.

Mary loved Jesus and trusted Him. Others scoffed at her presence, but Mary only spoke once in scripture that we can see; not to defend herself, but to mimic her sister's words. She felt no need to try to prove she was right. No need to defend her place. No need to correct or belittle others. She let Christ be her defender.

What a lesson for us to learn: measure our words and love extravagantly.

Get Real: Reflection & Prayer

1. Which part of the story of Mary of Bethany impacts you the most and why?

2. What did you learn from this Mary's story?

3. What is God teaching you about your tongue?

4. What do you need to do, say, or pray after reading this chapter?

5. Is there a distinction between defending yourself or your actions and being defensive?

6. How might being defensive sound or look? How might defending yourself or your actions sound or look?

7. How is this same issue of "defensive versus defending" important where our children and our spouses are concerned?

Father God,

Help me to learn the lessons You need me to learn as I read through the story of Mary of Bethany and her sister, Martha. I am seeking answers, looking deeper, and trying to live the lives You created me for, Lord. Help me to be still and soak You in.

In Jesus' name,

Amen.

CHAPTER 4

Staying Positive in a Negative Space

*"Finally, brothers, whatever is true, whatever is honorable,
whatever is just, whatever is pure, whatever is lovely,
whatever is commendable, if there is any excellence,
if there is anything worthy of praise,
think about these things."*
(Philippians 4:8)

REAL LIFE: Guilty Whys

The global pandemic forever changed our landscapes. Not that tragedies of the past have not changed us. Hurricanes, earthquakes, tsunamis, tornados, mass shootings inside public places, schools, and houses of worship have left us changed, divided, and broken. But the pandemic attacked the entire world at the same time — not just one region or place. Why does God allow bad things to happen? This is a question many non-believers, seekers, and Christians ask when they see things which seem tragically unfair.

The answer is easier than most people make it. This is not how God wanted it to be. What we now see was not what He created. Also, fully understand that the world has a Creator. It is not a happy accident of a Big Bang. Refuting and breaking that argument down to fact would be another book and there are many already published on the topic.[10]

So, what is the answer? Unfortunately, we now live in a fallen world. God's contract with man was broken in the Garden of Eden by Adam and Eve (Genesis 3). The Earth and God's creation are currently ruled by the prince of darkness known as Satan. Make no mistake, his job is to prowl about like a hungry lion looking for a fresh kill.

> *"Be sober-minded; be watchful.*
> *Your adversary the devil prowls around*
> *like a roaring lion, seeking someone to devour."*
> (I Peter 5:8)

Stress, anxiety, and fear are three of the enemy's favorite tools. He has used them since the dawn of time. He knows just how to fashion his traps around us to make perfect-fitting shackles and chains to paralyze us. Satan wants us to make bad decisions when we are stressed and become enslaved to anxieties and fear. The enemy also enjoys watching us beat ourselves up with negative self-talk, negative behaviors, and unhealthy mindsets and habits. If we beat our own selves up, he does not have to work as hard. Every hour we beat ourselves up is an hour he can use to focus on someone else.

As a child, I was born into an exceedingly difficult time in my parents' marriage and my mom's life. She had one chronically sick toddler and her father had died. She was not looking for another kid. My relationship with my mother was strained under the pressure. My parents divorced when I was four years old. She did the best she knew how to do, but I wish she had been better equipped. I was thirteen before I honestly remember my mother saying she loved me. I know she did in her own way, but my ears and my heart longed to hear those words from her more.

My mom was strong and had been through many battles in her life, but somewhere along the way, her strength turned into anger and a root of bitterness. She survived the shame of a first marriage that fell apart on her wedding night. As my grandmother told it, they did not approve of the older man she was seeing, but she ran off and got married anyway. After consummating the marriage, he went out for a loaf of bread and pack of cigarettes and never came back. I cannot imagine the embarrassment and betrayal she felt. I wonder how many times she asked herself what would have happened if she had listened to her parents.

She then took a liking to my father's cousin, but he was not interested. Soon she began dating my dad. He was a good boy from a good Christian home. The one time I asked her why she married him, she said, "I needed his goodness." I am not sure that is ever a great reason to get married. Her answer still baffles me. It was like somehow marrying my father would save her reputation, even though they lived in different towns. At the time of our discussion, she hated him and blamed him for everything she despised about men.

Their marriage produced the blessing of four girls, but the damage of constant fighting and multiple affairs led them to call it quits after fifteen years. She was a secretary with four kids and two failed marriages. My mother was charming, smart, and witty, but her anger at life and God were enormous.

Years later, she became the vice-president of a company and held her own in a man's world. I learned a great deal from her. Still, her brokenness and negative mindsets were always near the surface and unfortunately, without knowing it, I internalized them as a way of life for myself.

My childhood left me with scars that took decades of hard work to overcome. I had to be intentional in my healing. The enemy sucker-punched me with guilt and shame over choices that were out of my control. I felt guilty about my parents' divorce because my mom did not want me, and I was part of what led to the end of their marriage. Somewhere in my adolescent brain, I questioned what I could have done to make things better among the adults in my life.

This is a common problem. Children will wonder if their parents would have stayed married "*if only*" they had cleaned their toys or rooms better. Maybe you are still carrying baggage from childhood that you did not pack for yourself. Put it down and walk away.

My guilt compounded over stupid choices in college. I did well with school, but my personal choices went with the crowd, the night, and the availability of fun. Within a few years after college, I was married. Seven years later, I had a failed first marriage. His adultery and drug use caused me more guilt and shame. I went from carrying a suitcase of guilt and shame around college to toting a wheelbarrow of it after my divorce.

When Daryl died, my guilt and shame wheelbarrow turned into a truck load. What could I have done differently during his recovery? Why had I not heard him call out my name when his wheelchair turned over? What would have happened if I had just stayed in the room? Why did he not stay at the table like he promised he would? What if… what if… what if?

Girl, Stop.

Guilt is never of God. It is always a tool of the enemy. Hanging out on the playground of the enemy is not a good idea. He will go to great lengths to make it pretty and comfortable in his fenced-in park. If you find yourself inside the fences, do not stay. It is a trap. Get off the merry-go-round of shame, guilt, and what ifs. It is not how God wants you or me to live. How can we be "less than" if we are made by The Creator of the Universe?

Letting go of guilt around Daryl's death was without a doubt one of the most difficult things I have ever tried to do in my life. But, if I am who I say I am, then it could only be done by the hand of God while walking with like-minded people. Eventually, I realized I am not God and I did not get to pick how many days Daryl lived. There was nothing I could have done to add one more day to his life. The Bible says God knows the number of our days, and our times are in His hands. (Job 12:10, Psalm 139:16)

For as much as I wanted to believe I might have been able to save him, God picked the day Daryl went to Heaven. I was not to blame. The doctors were not to blame. Daryl was not to blame. God was not to blame, either. There was no blame, just a God-ordained time.

Eventually, I parked my truck load of guilt and shame at the foot of the cross and left it for God to move. His desire was not for my existence to be a black hole of negative mind space. I had to shift my mindsets and learn to not repeat the patterns I had seen growing up.

Nervousness and fear are not what He wants for us. Sadness and pain are the twin opposites of gladness and passion. If we did not experience deep sorrow and cutting pain, we would not fully understand the depths of mercy and the goodness and freedom of gladness or the euphoria of passion. But living in the positive spaces takes a mental shift and intentionality.

Girls, God wants us to walk in peace and leave our burdens with Him. He wants us to live in the fullness of His joy and the boundless potential of the purpose He made us for: our destiny. Imagine God asking you to set down your suitcase or truck load of fear, anxiety, negativity, shame, pain, work, failure, and frustration at His feet. When you let go, you feel so light and free you cannot believe it. The crushing weight leaves your shoulders, your heart, your mind, your gut; and you feel twenty pounds lighter.

Imagine yourself walking away for a minute or two. Stop. Turn around and wave goodbye to the mess you have left. Do not ever look back again, God's got it from here. He will clean it up. He will manage it. He will control it. Each time you feel yourself thinking about it, stop and pray. Ask God to remind you how far you have come and thank Him for taking over and letting you walk in His peace and comfort.

He will pick up this baggage for you. He's got you. He sees you. He loves you and will protect you.

> *"For I know the plans I have for you," says the LORD.*
> *"They are plans for good and not for disaster,*
> *to give you a future and a hope.*
> *In those days when you pray, I will listen."*
> (Jeremiah 29: 11-12, NLT)

Let it go and leave it with Him.

Run. Skip. Sing. Shout.

Like a child on a sunny day living their best life on God's playground, go have some fun. L-I-V-E!

REAL WOMEN FROM SCRIPTURE: MARY MAGDALENE

I loved Him, not like a follower loves and respects a rabbi, but with full abandon. With all of my heart, soul and mind…I loved Him. Jesus freed me from more than I can ever describe. I was bound and possessed; I was contorted and could be found filthy. I was spewing words that were not my own. I was shackled and tortured from within. I was a miserable captive.

I was a shadow of my own mind which never allowed me to be in full control of my own thoughts or actions. There was not a moment's rest. No peace, no joy, no way out of my tortured brain or body. I had no idea how or why this happened to me. Was it my parents' sin, my sin, or just an evil opportunity?

Why me? How long could this go on before it killed me? I was enslaved to the voices inside of my head.[11] I had no control over my body and mind, darkness and evil mastered them. There is only one Satan, one devil, but he has many minions and seven of them possessed me. I could not overpower them by myself. I was too weak to regain any command or normalcy. People were afraid of me.

That day, I followed the crowd down to the water's edge. There were many gathered there and so much noise. But as surely as I stood disheveled and worn, He saw me. Why? What drew Him to me? Was it the pure divinity of Jesus of Nazareth that clearly saw the evil inside me? Was it the compassion of a Father who wanted to rescue His child?

I do not know, and I do not care.

I do know that as soon as He commanded those demons to come out and leave me, I was FREE! Free from the torture, free from lies, free from captivity, free from bodily harm, free from the noise.

JESUS SET ME FREE!

I had never known peace like this. It was as if my filthy, worn out, patchwork dress was traded in for a beautiful silk robe. He made me new. He gave me breath. Not a shallow breath, but a deep breath like after a slow soaking rain when the air is clean and crisp with just a hint of sweetness as it fills your lungs. Jesus gave me this kind of breath. He gave me my life back and that gave me hope.

I made a choice in that moment to follow Him. No matter where He was going, I was going with Him. Even if He never spoke to me again, I would have followed Him just to be in His presence; to be near Him. Jesus was gracious, and we spoke often as I served Him.

My life of torment and torture was completely changed by just one of Christ's commands. Perhaps, when your life is literally saved by someone, your love for them is uncommon.

I am Mary Magdalene and I served Jesus without hesitation. I followed, listened, learned, and cared for Him. It was not a duty, but a privilege. I had been cast out and used by many, but not by Jesus.

One of my fondest memories came towards the end of His life. To prepare us, Jesus tried to explain what would happen in the near future. He told us He would not always be with us. I could not picture Jesus not being nearby. I couldn't fathom not hearing His voice anymore.

We could not comprehend how soon the day would come when the crowds would go from cheering Him as the King, and laying palm branches on the road before Him, to demanding His death. It frightened me. People were vicious and cruel.

Yet, the day came when He was arrested and shackled. They took Him from me; from us. I followed Him through the trial and judgment, listening to the mockery of it all. Everything they accused him of were lies, lies, and more lies! How could they?

Did they not understand He was not only a man, but the Son of God? Had they not heard of the miracles and wonders? Had they not seen my life change? Did they not know? Had they not heard the testimonies? I am one of many who had been healed by His hand.

There have not been words invented yet that are able to adequately describe the sound of a metal spike piercing the flesh of one you love. The noises repulsed my ears and swirled in my mind. The precision and pain were so perfectly placed as the spikes held His flesh to an upright tree without breaking the fragile bones.

Thud, thump, ting, bang, crack. He wailed…it was unimaginable horror.

Along with others who loved Him, I stood on the mountain they call Golgotha and watched Christ be crucified. Horror and disbelief collided on that wooden cross. He was held by spikes and beaten almost beyond recognition. His crucifixion beams hung between two common criminals. I wondered how He could love the world and its people so much when He knew His fate.

He had explained His life would somehow come to this. Until I stood heartbroken at that horrific scene, I did not fully understand or believe His words. What would happen next? Would those demons from long ago try to return to me? Would I be strong enough to battle them now? Would anyone ever believe He was who He said He was? Would anyone ever believe the miracle that happened to me?

The horror was real, but I also knew in my spirit - Jesus of Nazareth was the real Messiah. My heart ached so deeply, I felt like it would explode. I could not stop the overwhelming wave of emotions. Before I could process it all, the sky turned pitch-black, utterly dark, in the middle of the daylight hours.

As He took His last painful breath, the earth shook violently and the temple veil was torn.

I stood with His mom and cried.

JESUS!

I must have gone through a million tears and a thousand whys and what-ifs. Slowly following His mother Mary, I placed one foot in front of the other as I began to move towards His body. We were honored to care for Him one last time by preparing His body for burial.

Little did we know that His life had not actually ended that day, nor would His story. Just three days later, through more tears, I was shocked and amazed as I spoke with angels and cried out "Rabboni!" at the sight of the resurrected Jesus Christ. He was genuinely like no other god. The stone had been rolled away from the tomb and He was brought back from the dead. He came out of the grave and stood as the only living Savior. He died to save all mankind from their own sin and death, and yet He lived again.

The once broken, used, and enslaved Mary of Magdalene received such a blessing and place of honor from Jesus that first Easter morning. I ran as fast as I possibly could to tell everyone that Jesus Christ had risen. He was and is alive and the world will never be the same again! It was my news to tell!

Girls, Mary Magdalene went from demons to distinguished through the hand of Yeshua. Only through the life, the breath, the blood, and the resurrection of Jesus Christ could something like this happen. Just like it happened to her, it can happen to you. He is the only one that can offer complete healing to a life of utter brokenness. Mary Magdalene was mentioned fourteen times in the Gospels.[12] She loved Jesus and He loved her. Trust that He loves you too.

For more reading on Mary Magdalene, see Matthew 27:56, 61; 28:1; Mark 15:40, 47; 16:1-19; Luke 8:2; 24:10; John 19:25; 20:1-8.

REAL BATTLES: Negative Word Loops

Negativity is a habit. It is a mindset with old patterns. You may not even realize you have a tape playing in your mind, with negative thoughts or habits on a continual repeating loop. In my past, one of the comments I often heard was, "You are a fat slob." Sometimes it was, "You are a fat slob, and you will be a nobody for the rest of your life." I took this word from the person who spoke this to me as truth.

It. Was. A. Lie.

Do not let what someone else has called you have more authority in your life than what God calls you. Every single time you hear your negative loop start to play, stop it and speak God's truth over yourself and your life. God calls you names like "Daughter," "My Beloved," "My Child," and "Friend."

It took me years to learn how to stop playing these negative word loops in my mind. I struggled with my weight for many years and would binge eat and listen to this fat slob loop. I had to learn how to take my thoughts captive like Paul teaches us to do. Once I better understood this teaching, I would stop the negative lie and replace it with scripture.

> *"I praise you, for I am fearfully and wonderfully made.*
> *Wonderful are your works; my soul knows it very well."*
> (Psalm 139:14)

I don't know your lie, Girl, but I do know God has enough words that speak life to replace every single syllable you have ever believed as a false narrative in your mind or spirit. Find the scriptures you need and get to work replacing the negative patterns you have been listening to. Write them on cards or post-it notes. Post them around the house or keep them in your pocket. Make these scriptures available so you can quickly stop the negative loop with His Word.

REAL POWER FOR THE REAL WORLD: Mind Fields

Our brains have an easier time believing the negative things people say about us than the positive affirmations. The negative sticks like strong tape and leaves residue when we try to pull away. There is science and psychology out there to prove it, but consider the point from a simple perspective we see every day. We women deflect almost every compliment that comes our way.

>Them: "I like your dress!"

>Us: "Oh, I got this for half off" or "I picked this up at the secondhand store." Or "This old thing?"

>Them: "Thanks for the hard work."

>Us: "It was a team effort."

>Them: "You are pretty."

>Us: "I don't even have makeup on today. You are just being nice."

We have no idea how to manage compliments. Let an entire paragraph of positive things surround one negative or almost negative thing and what does our brain focus on most? You said it — the negative! Why did he say…? What did my boss mean by…? We will take one negative comment and turn it into an entire conversation in our mind, playing both parties in the conversation that is only happening inside our head. What a waste of energy and imagination!

We must get better at taking thoughts captive. Own them and be mindful instead of letting thoughts take you to dark places or keep you in bondage to them. You do not have to continue thinking about everything that comes into your mind. If you start to go down the rabbit hole of negative thoughts, stop your train of thought. Immediately ask God to help you. Take that thought captive, cast it away in Jesus' name, and then speak God's truths and stay positive.

If you have people around you who like to grumble and complain, gossip, and talk about how bad other people or certain things are, remove yourself from them. Staying around people who are spinning in the negative realm will cause you to get drawn in or lose your peace. Allow the Word of God to develop your faith to affect them more than they infect you.

Finally, spend time with God. Lean in and draw near to Him. Listen like you would lean into the whisper of your lover telling a good story, as if every nanosecond that matters comes from their next sentence and your next moment of togetherness. This is the kind of intimacy and proximity we need with God. This kind of relationship with Him keeps us out of the minefield of our minds and in the presence of the Holy Spirit.

Get Real: Reflection & Prayer

1. What are the emotions the enemy uses to attack you with? When do they get triggered the most?

2. What lies have you believed as a truth about yourself? What is something God calls you instead?

3. What would you like God to trust you with more of and how would you honor Him by sharing it?

4. Read Philippians 4:4-9, then take time to write it out below. As you do, ask God to help you replace your negative loops with His Word and His peace.

5. What situations or people do you need to approach more positively in your life and what is one way you can do it?

6. What are three things you can do when a conversation becomes negative?

7. What are two small/micro-habits you want to begin working on immediately?

Father God,

I surrender my thoughts to You. If they are wrong, replace them with right. If they are false, replace them with truth. Give me healthy mindsets of gratitude and peace. When I begin to go down the rabbit holes of negative thinking, stop me immediately and help me take my thoughts captive.

In Jesus' name,

Amen.

CHAPTER 5

Learning Discipline Takes Discipline

*"Whoever loves discipline loves knowledge,
but he who hates reproof is stupid."*
(Proverbs 12:1)

REAL LIFE: Food Has Been My Kryptonite

Healthy things grow, but in the past, my belly had grown way too much. It was not healthy. Self-control around food is an issue God has been working through with me for most of my life. Unfortunately, I do not have a shut-off valve when I begin eating. I really enjoy food and I grew up Southern.

Living in the South gives you a respect for multiple cultures and the diversity of their foods. Authentic tamales, Mexican and Latino flavors, Cajun cuisine, and soul food are just a few examples. I also have an appreciation for authentically fried foods, which, according to my grandmother, meant they had been cooked in yesterday's grease. Here in the South, too many of us live to eat instead of eating to fuel our bodies and live.

For me, somehow, food is tied to comfort and a bit of rebellion. I heard things like, "You have to clean your plate before you can leave the table. There are people starving around the world. Eat." I also heard things like, "You would be pretty if you lost a *little* weight."

Mealtime became an eating contest between me and my siblings. My afternoon snack became a family size bag of chips or an entire can of tuna. To keep me quiet on long road trips from Arkansas to Texas, my grandpa would buy me a bucket of chicken that I would eat mostly by myself, all…day…long.

I was overweight throughout my childhood. In third grade my best friend, Kara, took a picture of me on my bicycle and a big bulldog posing next to me. On the back, she wrote, "Who's who?" Yes, she is still my best friend decades and a million stories later. I chose not to take offense because she makes me laugh and she is one of the coolest people I know. Plus, the bulldog and I did have a similar amount of fat rolls and were both cute in our own ways.

During my freshman year of college, I gained so much weight. I was close to 180 pounds on a five-foot, one-inch frame. It meant I wore a size 18. I remember when my wellness check came back freshman year saying I was morbidly obese. The words were harsh, hard, real, and painful. They were also true. It was the first time anyone had ever held me accountable for my weight. I tried to make changes, but I was so clueless about nutrition. I thought switching to a fried chicken sandwich and tater logs was better for me than a hamburger and fries. It took an upper classman, in the lobby of the band building, explaining to me that fried chicken on a bun was not necessarily better than a burger before I began to realize how much I did not know about healthy eating.

That year, I caught the flu and lost ten pounds in a week. I knew if I was ever going to choose new foods and get healthy, this was the time to start. The flu set me on a journey of weight loss and exercise. Over a three-year period, I dropped to 103 pounds. My family thought I was anorexic. They had no idea what a healthy body weight was or what it should look like. My family's view of food was distorted and wrong. For the first time in my life, as a college sophomore, I was actually at a healthy weight for my frame. I had to realize when my view is distorted, I see truth as a lie.

Food has been my kryptonite. In the past, I have prayed, sought, and yo-yoed. Now, I speak truth about who I am and what I need to eat. I continually learn and grow in this area. But there are also days when I eat chips and salsa, so I restart and do better the next day. I have to be mindful about my food choices every single time I eat or the unhealthy food patterns my family taught will win.

Unhealthy bites today do not serve me wellness for tomorrow. They are not compatible with what I desire for my life or my health. I seek new and different mindsets and outcomes for my health and wellness. I am incredibly grateful that I now have a like-minded tribe to help hold me accountable and to do life with. I coach others on their own health journey as a way of holding myself accountable. It is not about showing off. It is about showing up for myself and others. It is about giving back what I have learned.

Whatever your area of self-control surrounds, make sure you are seeing it authentically. Perspective and vision can tie us to both healthy and unhealthy outcomes. Face your own kryptonite and take away its hold. It may not be food, drugs, or alcohol. Maybe it is wasted time, bad habits, negative thoughts, pornography, out-of-control spending, watching news that steals your joy, or something else. No matter its name, you have the power, through Jesus Christ, to control it instead of it controlling you.

We need time with God and good role models around us in order to develop better self-control and personal discipline. Time alone with God is vital for growing our relationship with Him. It is also a way to change our bad habits, negative patterns, and destructive loops.

Relationships take time. If we want to know the heart of God, we must spend time with Him. Through that time, we better learn to trust. When we trust Him, we begin to long to please Him above doing what we have always done or what feels good in a tempting moment. When we trust Him, He will help us make better choices on our way to new healthy habits.

REAL WOMEN FROM SCRIPTURE: LOT'S WIFE

I am a woman who loved my family and the land God had blessed us with. Our property dotted the plain of the Jordan River. It was a fertile land, lush with the wellsprings of life and the city bustled with busyness. This was our family's inheritance. It was our chosen land. Sure, there were rumblings in the family about our perceived selfishness because we had picked the best land out of the family inheritance. Abraham gave us the choice. So, we took it.[13] Were these rumblings anymore unusual than what happened in other homes? Grumbling, murmuring, complaining, and jealousy about choices family members make is common, right?

To me, this place was the perfect mix of city life and farming country. My husband, Lot, had green pastures to feed his cattle and make our living more lavish. I, on the other hand, had city life close by with its sights and sounds. The smell of bread baking, vendors selling their goods in the open market, festivals, music, and the bustle of daily life comforted me. It was a perfect location for each of us, and our family.

I loved my shrewd businessman who chose to make his living from the land. We had four beautiful girls with three yet to be married. But I knew the day would come when suitors would line up for our girls. We were a prominent family, but the girls were also still young. Their time would come. They did not yet realize their full worth by the world's standards, but I knew. Their father, my strong husband, was the nephew of Abraham. To our people, this bloodline mattered a great deal.

Lot was a wise and godly man whose family held much esteem among our tribes. We heard tales and had seen evidence of his uncle's encounters with God. God had spoken directly to his uncle and we knew this story well although this was a problem for us at times. Lot feared, loved, and served the Lord as an upstanding righteous man. He found it hard to live in this city I held dear. It was somehow not right for him to love the Lord and live with those who did not know Him or knew Him and chose to blatantly disobey His commands. I knew of his concern but wanted to stay here, at home.

Over the years, the city grew darker and more defiled. What started out as fun turned ugly. Theft, lies, wild parties, and sex with anyone and any thing became the norm. There were even tales of human sacrifice, orgies, and corruption at the highest levels. I knew they happened, but somehow it just seemed normal for us to make different choices than others and still live among them. I somehow ignored the severity or discounted it.

These evil things broke the heart of God. We had no way of knowing that Abraham was interceding with the Lord and his angels who were determined to destroy the city. Apparently, the wickedness was too much for God to bear any longer. Abraham pleaded with God on our behalf. The Lord finally agreed to spare the city provided ten righteous people could be found.

It was like any other evening; Lot was at the city gate and I was at home. He knew when the angels approached the gates that they were different. My husband pressured them to stay away from the dangers of the inner city and to stay at our home instead. I was not so sure this was a good idea, but inside our walls with us, they would be welcomed by my husband, fed, and have their feet washed. They wanted to stay in the town square, but Lot made them come to our house instead. Our home was well supplied and always had room for company.

The angels feasted and began to relax, but word of their presence had traveled quickly. Townspeople heard of these new men passing through and brought their wickedness to our front door. A mob of men, both young and old, gathered outside. They wanted our guests to join them in the town square for sex. My husband was appalled at their demands and threats of violence.

Lot went out, closed the door behind himself, and pleaded with the mob not to harm the men. They only became angrier. In a moment of desperation, he even offered our young virgin daughters to the mob. He thought it was somehow better that our daughters be taken than angels of the Lord. I was shocked. I wanted all these people to leave us alone. I could see no good way out of the mess.

The mob refused our daughters. Their anger rose as they tried to push past my husband. They were about to break down the door when our guests revealed their heavenly gifts. The two angels quickly opened the door and snatched Lot back into the house. Then they blinded the mob. The mob groped in darkness but could not find the door.

Seeing the debauchery, the angels of the Lord told my husband to gather our family and leave town immediately. They told him the Lord had removed His hand from this wicked city and it would be decimated. I loved this city. This could not be. Neither of us understood the severity of the warning. Lot tried to convince our soon to be sons-in-law to leave with us, but they too denied the warning was real.

Confused and exhausted, we laid down to rest for the night. Then something unexplainable happened. The angels awoke us before sunrise and urged us to flee. The city would be destroyed forthwith, and if we stayed, we would be swept away in the destruction. We clung so tightly to what we could see that we missed what we could not see. We did not fully listen and comprehend. Then it was too late. The angels brought us out of the city. They spared us, but we still tried to argue. They wanted us to go to the hills, but Lot urged them to allow us to go to the small city of Zoar.

There was no stopping the destruction as it rained down from the heavens. The command came forth from the booming voices of the angels. *GO! Do not look back and do not stay on the plains!* Furiously, we obeyed. We were almost to the safety of Zoar when my heart cried out. Behind me, I heard the crashing of brimstone. I smelled the singe of fire and burning flesh and heard the screams. The screams were heart-rending. I thought of my friends, the market, our home. What was happening?

I could not help myself. I simply wanted one last look; one tiny peek. Could I see any of those whom we loved [14] behind us? Had they changed their minds? Were they following us? I gasped for breath as I looked back for one last glance at my home. Then…all was lost. There was nothingness.

> *"The sun had risen on the earth when Lot came to Zoar.*
> *Then the LORD rained on Sodom and Gomorrah*
> *sulfur and fire from the LORD out of Heaven.*
> *And he overthrew those cities, and all the valley,*
> *and all the inhabitants of the cities,*
> *and what grew on the ground.*
> *But Lot's wife, behind him, looked back,*
> *and she became a pillar of salt."*
> (Genesis 19:23-26)

Girls, why did Lot's wife look back? Love for the city or love of the flesh—perhaps love of her neighbors, friends, or family— no one knows. That tale will never be told. Disobedience cost her everything.

What are you peeking at today? What has God set behind you that still holds too much of your attention? What door has God closed that you keep trying to pull open? Could it cause you to lose everything if you keep coming back to it? Is it just a distraction from the enemy to keep your mind away from what God has ahead for you? Obedience is hard, but its reward is great and does not lead to destruction. Stop looking over your shoulder. There is a reason why God placed those things behind you.

For a better understanding of Lot's wife and her story, read Genesis 18:22-19:29 and Luke 17:32-33.

REAL BATTLES: Old to New

What we need, instead of self-loathing, is some Spirit-led self-control (fruit of the Spirit). We need to grow past old habits and take new actions.

Self-control is about discipline and requires maturity and forethought. Sometimes it's easier than others. If we are honest, some *people* also make it easier than others. Lot's wife lost her self-control, and she paid the price with her life.

> *"Patience is better than power,*
> *and controlling one's emotions,*
> *than capturing a city."*
> (Proverbs 16:32, CSB)

Chances are self-control is needed somewhere in our lives each day. It may be needed in our emotions and moods, our mouths and words, our reactions and temper, our children and family members, our time and money, or our health. Though it will be challenging, the ability to control our impulses and make good choices helps our relationships, our jobs, our self-image, our well-being, our moods, and our faith. How can we gain self-control? By training ourselves in discipline and by putting some boundaries and order around our behaviors and actions.

Better choices and pattern changes strung together multiple times or days in a row will soon turn into new habits. Put away the cookies or chips and take a walk for five minutes. Get off your phone or social media and go outside for ten minutes instead. Stop talking about someone else and write, pray, or work on yourself instead. Build new habits and patterns little by little and they will stick. Soon, the old becomes new.

REAL POWER FOR THE REAL WORLD: Micro-Habits

Invest time in studying what God says about the habits you want to better control. Then be intentional about praying for those new habits. Prayer is an offensive weapon in the Kingdom of God. It has the power to change things.

None of us can change through our own strength. We are not that smart, that strong or that good. It takes God in the middle of us to bring about lasting changes. He can change us quicker than we ever can. Our best efforts are not nearly as good as His.

Consider this: if you want to read your Bible more, put it next to your bed and start with one verse a night. As that becomes habit, increase to two verses or five minutes. Just add a small new habit that is still easily achievable. If you want to write or journal more, put your journal and pens or your laptop/tablet on your desk or next to your TV. Before you check emails or turn on your TV, spend two minutes writing. Again, do this small thing every day until it becomes natural, then increase the time by a couple of minutes and continue the positive habit.

Why should you start micro-habits instead of setting a goal to read a chapter a night or reading for thirty minutes? Because micro-habits set us up for long-term sustainable change. They are easily achievable, and this makes you feel good about staying on target. Once they become a habit, just add on a few minutes and build up your endurance.

There is a ton of research available on habits and micro-habits. Find an author you like and start reading. You will learn how little changes can lead to powerful transformation.

Get Real: Reflection & Prayer

1. What area(s) of life do you need to leave behind and stop looking back at?

2. What self-control issues have you overcome during your life? How did you move past them?

3. In the story of Lot's wife, what did you consider from a new viewpoint?

4. What new habits would you like to develop?

5. What will or could be your reward for building new and better habits?

6. Write out Titus 2:11-12.

7. Write out Galatians 5:22-23 and consider which attribute you want to work on most.

Father God,

Help me to become a woman with discipline and self-control. Help me find ways to form new and healthy habits. Give me grace with myself as I learn how to grow past old mindsets. Keep Your hand upon me. Help me to prune away the unhealthy mindsets of the past. Help me to focus on and pursue self-control, the fruit of the Spirit.

Make me new, Lord.

In Jesus' name,

Amen.

CHAPTER 6

Love...It's Complicated

*"With all humility and gentleness, with patience,
bearing with one another in love,
eager to maintain the unity
of the Spirit in the bond of peace."*
(Ephesians 4:2-3)

REAL LIFE: Marriage Is Hard

There is no way to sugar-coat this—developing a good marriage is hard work. The communication and compromise involved can be both difficult and time consuming. It can be mentally exhausting sometimes, but girls, when it is good, there is nothing like it in the world. Nothing. It is a blessing to come home to someone who loves you. Having that special person to do life with who has chosen you and truly respects you is a gift you should never take for granted.

So how do we make sure our marriages are good? How do we live in unity?

Many women's devotionals talk about being a Proverbs 31 woman. While I strive to have the traits and characteristics of the woman described in Proverbs 31, I also recognize two things. First, it is a grueling list, and second, to become more like her, I personally need a Proverbs 31 kind of husband. What's that? For me, it's a resilient mate who can encourage, support, run alongside me, and love me well. A Proverbs 31 man is not a husband I have to drag along beside me or carry because he is too weak to shoulder life's load. Being a pack mule for past hang-ups and hurts would not make me want to become a better human being or mate.

A Proverbs 31 husband must be strong and secure in himself to honor and respect his wife and her work. A Proverbs 31 man shows himself as a godly leader and example both within his home and to the outside world. I feel like we are out of balance in American culture when it comes to men leading our homes, our marriages, and our churches. It appears many men have left the church and/or left their families. Women have taken leadership roles in these places and do an amazing job. But sometimes I look around and wonder where the masses of godly men with integrity, self-respect, and passion for Jesus have gone.

Why aren't more couples walking into our churches together or worshiping side-by-side in house church? Marriage is a merging of two people into one unit. Couples need space to be independent, but they also need safe spaces to work on being together in a healthy way physically, emotionally, and spiritually.

Being together under one roof complicates preexisting communication issues, financial stressors, and the balance of emotional and mental wellness. We need each other, strong mentors, and a faith tribe to make marriage flourish. What may be a struggle for one independent person can sometimes become a larger or highlighted struggle for a couple, unless they can support each other and provide stability that will bring about both growth and change. Ideally, a good relationship and marriage grows and develops both people. Conversely, a bad relationship or marriage can cause one or both partners to regress, become stagnant, or codependent.

A union of two people becoming one unit is complex. Consider some questions newly married couples grapple with: *How will we have hard conversations if we cannot take a break from them and step away? Will we fight all the time? Who will take the lead on the big and small issues? Will we have children? Who will discipline the children and how will it be done? Can we make it and be financially secure? Does my spouse like me? Do they love me?*

Marriage makes us ask so many questions. Add outside pressures onto these and the relationship can easily crumble without a good support system or a solid foundation.

I earnestly believe the stress of quarantine brought on many more questions, cases of abuse, and trauma than we will ever know. My fear is that we will see the massive long-term toll lockdown took for years to come, not only on marriages, but on children. I could not imagine having little ones or being young in a marriage that was only in years three through seven during all the changes of 2020.

Those early years of married life can be complex. Often, there are times of deep personal growth for women as individuals, as well as for their roles of mom and wife. The changes can be strenuous without added chaos. The pressure cooker of the 2020 lockdown surely brought on much more stress and struggle. If you made it through, Girl, good for you. If you did not, learn and grow, find and give grace, and remember God is not done with you yet.

For the sake of discussion and reflection, let's consider my earlier statement about needing more godly men in America as we reflect upon marriage. It seems to me many TV sitcoms and shows since the 70's or 80's mock American men. The male characters often appear dumb, incapable, inept, and weaker than most of the women portrayed around them.

This was not always the case. For years, our society portrayed admiration and respect for strong men. These admirable men appeared intelligent in the ways of the world or in academics. They were the brave righters of wrongs done to women and children. They were respected and respectful to others, innately wise, givers and takers — not just takers and players.

As the world began to celebrate strong women too, it seems a lot of men walked away and tuned out. Absentee fathers became a normal occurrence. Many women raised families with no men/fathers present on purpose and/or by choice. It was easier for some women to have the children they wanted and bring them up alone instead of trying to take care of their babies alongside grown men who were acting like little boys. Grown men shrugging responsibilities and causing emotional damage became too common. Maybe it is easier to walk away when someone is not dependent upon you. I do not understand all of this, but I do recognize that somewhere down this road of lost and lonely people, strong turned into a trait of women and survivors, not just men in our culture.

I come from a long heritage of strong women who benefited by equality. I am not bashing women or women's rights, trust me. I respect the strength. I live the strength out loud. It is a core part of who I am. I totally understand that if I were born in another country, I may not have the same rights and options I had growing up as a woman within the borders of the USA.

However, after getting out of the trailer park where I grew up, my perceptions about men and their strength were tainted by the entertainment I watched, and by what I had seen play out before my eyes. Strong men do not have to be muscular or loud. They do not have to be big or tall. Those traits are not the only strengths, or definers of strength, a man can possess. My perception of marriage was also tainted. It took me a long time to understand marriage is a choice every minute of the day, not a feeling.

Marriage is not the dream wedding or the fairytale love story. Although both can be had, they are not marriage. Marriage is what comes after the honeymoon. It is the daily decisions. It is doing the right thing in a tempting moment. It is a choice to do the work, to respect one another, to stay in it and grow. It is a choice to let each other be strong and to become stronger together. It is a choice to not bully your mate verbally or physically. It is a choice to do what is best for both of you—not just one of you. Marriage is a choice.

We place too much emphasis on how we feel. Our spouse is not in charge of our joy. Feelings will let us down and toss us about. They can drown us through the unseen forces of their undercurrents. They cannot be the only factors for our happiness or for a divorce.

Marriage is about being loyal and faithful to God and each other even on days when we are not feeling it. If we look at the definition of faithful and examine our actions within our marriage against that definition, we may find the root of some marital problems.

Faithful: adjective [15]

- Strict or thorough in the performance of duty
- True to one's word, promises, vows, etc.

- Steady in allegiance or affection; loyal; constant
- Reliable, trusted, or believed
- Adhering or true to fact, a standard, or an original; accurate

Are we thoroughly active in our marriage each day? Are we staying true to our vows and promises, to love, honor, cherish, and care for our spouses in sickness and in health? Are we steady, loyal, reliable, and believable with a united front? Are we and our spouse able to answer "Yes" to all of these questions? If not, where are we being unfaithful and how can we fix it? Faithful is not a feeling, it is an attribute.

Marriage is complicated. It can be a beautifully choreographed dance sequence in which each partner gets their moments in the spotlight. The movement healthy couples create together is breathtaking and graceful. Marriage can also be indescribably hard, delicately fragile, and so infringing and violent when wills and bodies collide. This unhealthy dance, in distrust and darkness, leaves the floor covered with blood, sweat, and tears that no one sees until the spotlight comes back up and the partners have left the floor.

Marriage is a choice, so pick wisely. Your dance partner matters. The music they enjoy swaying to matters. Find someone who has God's heartbeat as their cadence, your song as their favorite jam, and desires to dance with perfect timing.

REAL WOMEN FROM SCRIPTURE: NOAH'S WIFE

Lately, I have looked around for Noah so many times and he is nowhere to be found. Where is he? People are starting to ask questions and I do not have the answers. Why does he hide from me and work for so long without a break? He is old, some 600 years old, and yet he works and toils away with the vision God has given him. Me? I have chosen to stand in silent support. He is my husband.

Could you imagine being me? In your old age, you watch your husband who is well up in years, begin to build a massive boat. He works day and night. He is scoffed, mocked, and yelled at all the time. Everyone thinks he has lost his mind, but he doesn't listen to them. He doesn't care what they say, he only cares what God says. He has an urgency for this mission. He cannot ignore it, even when it seems silly and a total waste of time to the whole village.

He has gone over his plans with me time and again. He has told me what he believes God is saying. I have watched this for years, asked thousands of questions, gone back over it all and still do not fully comprehend it. I know if he is right, then very soon we will be heartbroken, and nothing will ever be the same again. I don't understand it all, but I believe he thinks it is true.

I am trying to be patient and take care of our household. None of this makes any sense, but he will not let it go. I cry silent tears and just try to hang on to hope. He secures, shapes, and molds wood with every moment of his time and every ounce of his strength. His hands are worn and calloused. He says the plans are laid out by God and he cannot turn back now because he has come too far.

I try to love him better and trust his calling but some days, it is daunting. I miss his presence in our home. I miss talking to him and just being by his side. Sometimes, he works so late into the night that he does not even come back to the house. But he is still my husband, and he is a good man, no matter what.

I try to prepare myself and our belongings for whatever comes next. If we lose everything like Noah says, what will happen? What do we need to take with us, and what do we just leave behind? I talk with my sons and my daughters-in-law and help them prepare. We have decided to do this together as a family. There is so much to be done during this awkward transition.

Is he right?

Is the world about to be destroyed by water? Will it all be gone?

Then the day arrives when the biggest boat ever constructed is completed. The ark is ready, but part of me still wonders if I am. We begin to gather the animals. Many come two-by-two, and some by sevens; very big and small animals, fast and slow ones, ones that crawl, ones that fly. Animals that walk and swim—we have every kind because God Himself commissioned all of this.

The preparation and work is endless. We have an abundance of creatures to care for. How will we ever do this? My mind often begins to race. Everything seems impossible and so overwhelming.

Hurry!

Noah says we must hurry. There is urgency—almost a desperation—in his voice. He knows the time is upon us.

Soon the dire need he had felt became astonishingly clear. It is more than I imagined. I am utterly shocked. The water has come. It rose so quickly! It is hard to describe, there is no time left. He said this would happen, but to see it, to witness it, is surreal. Everything we had ever known is being overtaken, destroyed, and washed away by the power of nonstop water.

The gushing noise of the rising water is so incredibly loud. I have never heard anything like this in my life. Wait. Were those screams I heard? People are screaming in fear!

YAHWEH!

What will become of us? I cannot think of the horror or the pain I feel. Instead, I must trust and focus on how we survive and care for what we have been given. God has entrusted my husband and our family with so much. He has spared us. We have no idea what happens next, but we must obey Him and protect the animals. It is our duty.

There is no time nor need to grumble or complain. No time to focus on what we do not have anymore. I cannot look back and hold on to the past. I only have enough energy to look at what is before me. All I can do now is make plans for how we manage it, obey, and follow through.

We have been given a job; a God-designed mission. My husband heard God clearly and obeyed His commands even though it looked senseless and wasteful. We must have no fear, no doubt, no worry. We must work, trust, and have grateful hearts.

I am humbled my family is beside me.

I am a survivor.

I am a rebuilder.

I am Noah's wife.

Girls, have you stood by your man when the world was calling him names? Have you come home to an empty house because he was working late to provide? Have you thought, "Are any of his dreams actually possible?" What can you learn from the story of Noah's wife and her level of commitment?

For more information on Noah's wife and their story, read Genesis 6:18, 7:1-13, 8:16-18.

REAL BATTLES: Divorced & Widowed

One of my life's regrets is being married at 27 and divorced by age 33. My first marriage was a monumental failure and a tragic tale that I will try to unpack in some ways here. My ex-husband had a child without me while we were married. He loved drugs, alcohol, and lying more than he loved me or himself. I was clueless, arrogant, and immature, which made me too young for a lifelong journey. I had no business getting married and certainly no business getting married to him.

I did not understand the red flags I saw, but in sharing some of my story, I hope it impacts you or makes a difference for someone you know or may share it with. Although I learned valuable lessons from my failed marriage, I hated myself for my divorce. Honestly, I also hated God at times. Do not be shocked. I am not the first one to struggle with God. It was the ugly truth. God was big enough to manage my anger and He was extremely gracious, because He loved me back into Himself.

Even during the epic failure of a first marriage, I actually loved being a wife. I just made a bad choice for a partner. I overlooked things and thought the fact that he "needed" me was good. I could help him. I was probably arrogant enough to think I could "fix him".

What I learned was fixing myself—working on me—is all I can really do. I cannot be someone else's Holy Spirit. It is between them and God to become who God intends them to be, no matter how much I want to help. I cannot make them make better choices or do the right things.

I cannot personally save or fix a grown man. It is not my job. I am not a savior.

Honestly, the initial bad choices that got me into the marriage in the first place were on me. They were my fault. I knew who God was, but I ignored His truths in my early twenties. I tried to live with one foot in the world and one foot on the cross. You can party and have "fun" but go to church and pretend, right? It never worked for me and it will not work for you either. The world will always spin, you will lose your footing, and you will fall into its abyss.

Rarely does the tale of a good and lasting marriage start with "we met in a bar." I literally kicked my ex-husband out of a bar for being drunk and belligerent. I was the manager, the bartender, and a pit bull with a bite. The day after I threw him out, he came back to apologize. He was charming and could talk a good game and my twenty-something-year-old self believed his lies. Grown men in my world never said, "I am sorry." So, when he did, I bought it. Not long after the apology, we began dating.

Because I knew what was right, I eventually asked him about his faith and church. He told me his fondest memories from childhood were from church, VBS, and summer camps. I asked if he wanted to go with me sometime and he agreed. Remember that one foot on the cross and one foot in the world thing I mentioned earlier? I knew better.

When I tell you that we lived like Hell on Friday and Saturday but showed up on Sunday for some Jesus time, I am not exaggerating. I would bartend all week and cuss like a sailor; then show up on a Sunday to try and get something straight in my life. I was so lost on what it meant to be a grown up and what it meant to be a follower of Jesus.

Unfortunately, I had no clue my ex was a functioning addict. I knew he liked to smoke weed occasionally and drink. I was okay with that even though it was not my thing. I did not do drugs or have any desire for them, so why would I date someone who did and why would I marry him? I literally have no answer for that except I glossed over the sin and looked at the good parts I saw with my own eyes, instead of asking the Holy Spirit to help me see. I now know this was not okay.

I compromised my standards so I would not be alone and so I could help him be "better". I assumed he would leave all his bad behaviors behind when we got married and moved to a new city. He did not. I was naïve, young, and oblivious to what drug addiction really meant. I had no idea how many lies surrounded that lifestyle.

I cannot tell you how many times I have prayed for forgiveness. I know God forgives the first time if we earnestly repent and seek Him, but I have wrenched myself through the memories of my poor choices thousands of times. In hindsight, this marriage should never have happened. He was twelve years older than me, and somewhere in my young adult mind, that meant he was smarter than me. It meant he could earn a good living for us and we would be secure. These were false narratives. I found myself in the middle of something I never could have imagined.

Here is an example. One day, the phone rang and a voice on the other end said, "I know you don't know who I am, but I have your husband's baby."

I replied, "Then I guess I should know your name."

Once she told me her name, I repeated it out loud. No sooner had the words left my mouth than he came up off the couch like a cheetah pouncing on the first gazelle it had seen in weeks. In two steps he made it across the living room and snatched the phone out of my hands. Straightaway, I knew it was true.

We always had financial trouble even though I made good money. I had to sell my car to keep our electricity on and find a ride home from the car lot because he was nowhere to be found. Lawsuits piled up against him and his small business. Story after story could be told. When I finally had a clear view of the chaos we were in, I saw that I had not helped him become "better" in any authentic way. I had only helped him hide and appear more normal to the outside world. From the inside, I knew I was in a mess of a marriage to a cheating drug addict, but there was still nothing in me that wanted to be divorced.

When I was a little girl, never once when someone asked me what I wanted to be when I grew up, did I say "divorced." I had lived through it and knew what it did to families and their kids. I became incredibly angry and bitterly disappointed in him and his choices. Then I became angry at myself, and at God. The third time I tried to put him through a drug rehab program, he stayed three days, checked himself out, and went to his new girlfriend's house. Again, I was clueless. I thought he was still there at the treatment facility.

I paid his child support, set up our counseling, and asked our church family to become involved in his accountability. I did everything I could to set him and us up for success. Don't get me wrong, I was not perfect or faultless. My mistakes were too numerous to count, but I desperately wanted our marriage to work. And even after all of it, I was committed to staying married.

The last straw, after years of deception, was when I caught him trying to lie to me about a steam pipe burn on his hands that had left all of his fingers injured. It turned out that they were burns from a crack pipe that exploded in his hands. Not long after that lie, God woke me up incredibly early one morning and I just knew I was supposed to go find my spouse. I had no idea where to look because he had not come home in weeks. I just began driving toward his workplace which was over thirty minutes away. At a stoplight across the street from his building, I spotted him. He was pulling into the parking lot. It was all God's perfect timing. There was no other way for both of us to end up there at that exact moment.

I pulled up alongside him as he was getting out of his truck. I opened my window and asked him for the truth. "For seven years of my life, don't you think you owe me seven seconds of truth? Are you having an affair?" He hung his head like a five-year-old who had been caught stealing cookies. Finally, something inside me snapped into place.

When he lifted his head, he said the last word I ever heard him speak, "Yes." I was done. He was an addict and I hated myself with him more than I hated divorce. I told him I would file that day and he would receive papers soon. I had Biblical and earthly reasons, and our marriage was over, but that did not make it easy.

There is obviously a lot more history, so much brokenness, and a great deal of self-loathing. I would love to tell you that I left that day and clung to God, but I didn't. My anger and disappointment led me to a dark hideous place. I was so bitter that I literally shook my fist at Heaven and told God out loud, that I would get back to Him. I was making an ignorant choice to walk away from my faith and my Father because of my failed marriage; like it was God's fault. It is only by His grace that I am still here to write this story.

God is good, Girls, even when we are not. He is faithful even as we fail. He owes us nothing and gives us everything. It took a long time for me to crawl back towards intimacy with God, but eventually I began to pray again and believe He would hear and answer. What I still did not understand was how God was always listening, but His answers did not always look like the ones I wanted.

A few years later, when I was at the end of myself, a dear friend told me I should try a new church she kept hearing about. I knew she was right. I had been mad at God long enough and living without Him was not a choice I wanted to make forever. I needed a church family and accountability. I went to the place she suggested, and immediately knew I had found my place of healing.

It was a church that looked for broken people to restore through the power of Christ. It was in the middle of that warehouse church where I began working on me and restoring my relationship with God. It was also where I met Daryl Cox, a man whom I would eventually marry.

We became friends with no intention of anything more. We began talking easily and laughing a lot. He was a drummer and I am a vocalist. We had similar interests and I got his jokes, while apparently most other people did not. He treated me with respect and as an intellectual equal. We had people ask us when we were going to start dating and our reply was always, "never." We had both been wounded deeply by failed marriages and did not need or desire any extra drama.

However, after about ten months, there was no denying what we were beginning to feel. God was so obviously in it, so we began to seriously talk about remaining friends or taking the next step. After a conversation with the worship pastor and the youth pastor a few weeks later, we finally broke down and went to our founding pastor to seek wise counsel.

We sought wise counsel from an outside perspective to figure out if we should start dating or never cross the line. We both had enormously large amounts of baggage and no desire to hurt one another or be hurt again. Were we compatible? Was there even a possibility of it working? After a few sessions, the answer was "Yes."

By age 35, I was married to a man who made me want to become a better human being for myself and others. We had an amazing eleven years. I know, only eleven years. If I had finally learned what a good marriage is and worked to become healthy and whole, why only eleven years? Because, three months before our tenth wedding anniversary, Daryl died very unexpectedly.

I was widowed. He was gone and I was shattered. Marriage had been redeemed for me. I had finally discovered how God intended it to work and yet I was alone…again. I hated the word "widow(ed)" for a long time. Then I learned to make peace with the love story it told.

Grief was the price I paid for loving and being loved mightily. I would not take it back. I changed for the better during those eleven years. I stood hand-in-hand with a man of integrity who treated me respectfully. His patience and wisdom helped mend my heart. His encouragement helped me get my God roar back.

During the silence of the years following Daryl's death, I began to dissect what I had learned about love and partnership from two drastically different marriages. Let me try to lay out the lessons for you.

My first husband left me scarred and said things that still ring in my mind on bad days, "You've gained too much weight. I am not attracted to you anymore." My late husband frequently stopped mid-sentence, turn his head sideways and say, "You're so pretty." Then he would pick his sentence back up and go on with his story. Their perspectives of my body were different. Their words and treatment of me was vastly different.

My first husband stole money from our accounts and wasted it on other women and drugs. Daryl was honorable with money and respected healthy boundaries around it and me. His money worked for him and he was not enslaved to it or for it. I was his partner, his equal, not his bond servant carrying around all the things he dropped or fixing everything he broke.

My first husband did not like or respect himself so he could not even begin to love me in a healthy way. He lied when the truth actually sounded better because he was so used to living lies. My late husband lived by a code of ethics and expected me to do the same. He loved me well.

These are some of the lessons I learned during divorce and widowhood. I'm sure many of you have stories, too. Please learn to tell them, because somewhere out there, there is a girl who needs to hear about you and your journey. I am grateful for the lessons and the ability to figure out what healthy relationships and marriages should be like.

Divorce is not easy, but it is forgivable, because there is no condemnation in Christ. Grief is not easy either, but it is survivable. And, you never know what is on the other side of the valley of the shadow of death. God still had surprises in store for me and He does for you too.

REAL POWER FOR THE REAL WORLD:
Run Away If He Needs to Be Fixed

Girls, you cannot fix a guy. You cannot change him. You cannot save him. Do not choose a partner who needs to be fixed, changed, or saved. He must want to do these things for himself. Changing someone is not your job. You can rescue a puppy from the pound if you want to fix, save, or change something, but do not get seriously involved with a guy who "needs" you for this kind of work, especially if you need some fixing of your own. The only person you can ever change is you. You can impact other people's lives but changing is their work to do.

Find someone who is whole and healthy by being whole and healthy yourself. Being a whole and healthy person is really a superpower. If you are whole and healthy, you will attract whole and healthy. If you are a broken hot mess, you will attract a broken hot mess. I wish I could have understood this idea without having to go through the carnage of a failed marriage.

The woman described in Proverbs 31 can be an example for us all, no matter our level of education or dreams for our future selves. She is a good reflection of a godly woman within a godly household. If we use the practical examples of her qualities and work on them a little at a time while asking God to bring us transformation, we will make progress in our personal growth and our faith journey.

The great news is God loves us just the way we are right now, but He also loves us too much to let us stay this way. He wants us to rise up to the next level. He gives us second chances on our epic failures and on days when we mess things up. He also longs for us to persevere and keep growing in the areas where we are not living up to His desires and plans for us.

My image is not supposed to look like my best self. It is supposed to look more like Jesus. My tongue, my tone, and my words are places where God urges me to keep growing.

What are the places where you still need to mature?

Where does Jesus want you to look more like Him?

Get Real: Reflection & Prayer

1. How would you rate your marriage and why? If you are single, what do you find are the most important characteristics for your future spouse?

2. What are your thoughts surrounding the story of Noah's wife and the perspective of this writing?

3. What are the lessons God is trying to teach you about grief, loss, and loving better?

4. What are three practical things you can do to love better today?

5. What is working in your marriage and what is not? If you are single, what do you need to work on in yourself to attract the kind of mate you want?

6. Read Proverbs 31 and list her traits. What are the easiest and most difficult attributes for you?

7. We all need role models and godly examples. Who are the people in your community, workplace, or church who can be mentors and role models for you as you learn and grow? List their names and make an effort to reach out to them soon.

Father God,

Please help me today as I strive to work on the character traits of a godly woman. I long to live with faithfulness to You and those You call me to love. Mend broken relationships. Heal marriages in trouble and help me to be what You need me to be for each situation. Give me peace and joy in my home as I strive to be more like the description of a Proverbs 31 woman. Help me hold fast to You, Father.

In Jesus' name,

Amen.

CHAPTER 7

The Flesh Wants: Living in My Spirit Instead of My Feels

"No temptation has overtaken you that is not common to man. God is faithful, and he will not let you be tempted beyond your ability, but with the temptation he will also provide the way of escape, that you may be able to endure it."
(I Corinthians 10:13)

REAL LIFE: Self-Control?

Remember when I said earlier that you might be surprised by what is on the other side of grief and loss? In the spring of 2020, I married my forever love — we had the shortest and most attention-grabbing engagement ever. Then I epically failed during the onset of my first, and hopefully last, global pandemic. I will tell the incredible way God wove my husband Bryan and I together a bit later but let me start with a glimpse at our lockdown time.

Just like many of you during that spring, I quickly bought all the necessary items required to survive an unexpected and unknown global pandemic: hand sanitizer, toilet paper, paper towels, disinfectant wipes, cleaning supplies, bottled water, various kinds of tea (because it's my favorite), canned meats and vegetables, nonperishable foods and snacks.

By no means was this a comprehensive or wise list of "necessary supplies." Since I didn't have a checklist for global pandemic prep, I did the best I could. I packed my car with the greatest of geometric and spatial reasoning for maximum capacity. (Go math nerds!) Then I began my fourteen-hour drive across the country to get to my new love.

We had been married for nine days. Yes, nine days, before the first lockdown started, and had only been together for two of them. He surprised me on a Sunday in early March with an engagement and a wedding on the same day. He then flew back home on Tuesday. Bryan had to go back to work on a military base over 900 miles away from our wedding site.

As I loaded my car full of these "necessary supplies" to take from my apartment to his house, I was riddled with unknowns. I tried to pass the time with audio books and music. Around hour four of the journey, I became aware of the endless snack supply I had on hand. Discipline? What did it mean in such a time of uncertainty? Does discipline count in a pandemic?

In my normal world, I am the girl who gets picked on for my healthy snack choices. My friend Gina Radke tells me my food "smells like lies," because it's always healthy but smells like yummy deliciousness when I'm cooking. She smells burgers with bacon, but I have ground turkey cooked with a handful of veggies or a spaghetti squash. It's really all about the spices.

Some of my favorite snacks are turkey jerky, beet or kale chips, almond butter, and salt and vinegar almonds. These are the nibbles I crave and take on adventures. I've literally packed beet chips, dried coconut chips, and tuna in backpacks to take overseas to the Dominican Republic. One never knows when a snack will be required. The way to keep your team from eating ALL your snacks is to buy things you like that they refuse to eat or even taste.

For some reason, my friends believe a beet chip tastes "like dirt." I disagree. I actually talked a six-year-old into trying them one afternoon in the mountains of the Dominican. This kid had been working and playing hard all day. His dad ran our mission station and had told him not to ask for drinks or food from the team. I was sitting at a picnic table eating turkey jerky and beet chips, when Justus came and plopped down opposite of me, dutifully drinking his water.

The kid looked at me sideways with his brown curls and huge brown eyes. They were obviously unfamiliar snacks, and none of my team was diving into them. I handed him a beet chip and he ate it, ever so slowly. I said, "Do you want another one?" He politely declined, by shaking his head no. I laughed, but he was still game to try the turkey jerky, so the beet chip could not have been that bad. Proud to say turkey jerky was a score. Even six-year-old boys know it is legit jerky and mighty tasty.

So that's an example of my normal world of wellness eating. Then there was the beginning of the global pandemic when my brain thought it would be a good idea to buy things my new husband might like. I stocked up on peanut butter crackers, chips and dip, trail mix, canned peaches, chips, chocolate, gelatin snacks, chips, raisins, breakfast bars, and some MORE chips. Surely this would make him happy, right?

Oh, Teri…

Once I arrived at his home and began to unload, I realized *how much* I bought. And how amazing I really am at packing a car. By the end of week three, we needed groceries because, for the first time in many years, we were both eating three large meals a day along with lots of snacks. Even though we were both teleworking, somewhere in our minds it had turned into a childhood Christmas vacation. We stayed in our pajama bottoms, watched Netflix, put puzzles together, and ate ALL the chips and dips I had brought.

I may be the first woman in the history of marriage to gain ten pounds within the first five weeks of wedded bliss. I am also probably the first woman to discover a love of hot and spicy crackers covered in cheese powder on an unexpected weeks-long lockdown honeymoon. Prior to the pandemic, I had no idea these little crunchy squares of spicy, fake-cheesy goodness existed. As I made out the grocery list during week three, I had to check the cheesy cracker supply to see if we still had an abundance. Like, somehow, they should be written on the "necessary supply" list.

Where was self-control? Even though it was a stressful and abnormal time, self-control should have been practiced at some point. I am sad to say, with a great deal of confidence, I did not stop eating for about six weeks. I gained weight, felt miserable about myself, and came out of that time facing summer shorts season.

To have self-control, we must battle our own temptations. Sometimes it is a civil war between our mind and our heart's desires. Luke talks about how we must deny ourselves daily and take up our cross. (Luke 9:23b) What is your cross? Is it a mental battle, a physical battle, a spiritual or bodily battle? Each of us has a war to wage and if we wage it against ourselves, it is an interesting and intriguing battlefield, but one guaranteed to have carnage left behind. This is what the enemy wants. If we fight against our own self and self-worth, he does not have to work as hard.

The flesh wants what it wants, and most of the time, it wants it NOW. When we indulge the flesh and feed it with food, drugs, alcohol, pride, money, anger, hate, pornography, illicit sex, or any other desire that does not lead us toward God, we are on dangerous ground. Our feelings and body will often lead us to places our spirits would not go. Beware, Girl, beware.

REAL WOMEN FROM SCRIPTURE: POTIPHAR'S WIFE

"And as she spoke to Joseph day after day, he would not listen to her,
to lie beside her or to be with her.
But one day, when he went into the house to do his work
and none of the men of the house was there in the house,
she caught him by his garment, saying, 'Lie with me.'
But he left his garment in her hand and fled and got out of the house."
(Genesis 39:10-12)

How dare he not yield to me? A servant who will not give me what I want? It is a direct and outright violation and rare in my world. Does he not know my husband and tales of his power? As Commander of the Royal Guard, he has authority. He has a lot of pull and muscle. In quiet corners full of whispers, people call him "the chief butcher". He is not afraid of making hard choices and taking care of those who get in his way. My husband is a warrior.

How dare this domestic man defy me in my husband's house. Joseph is not like us. He is from a foreign land, handsome and young, ruddy. When he came to us, he was in his teens; just a boy really, but now he is a fully-grown man. His people, the Israelites, serve us Egyptians as slaves. I own him. He is my property and yet he said, "No" to me.

I cannot comprehend it. Never has anyone I owned dared to defy me in this way.

Every day, he served in our home and gained a little more power of his own. My husband, Potiphar, trusted him and gave him free reign of his household affairs. Me? I became obsessed with his figure walking in and out of my doorways.[16] He was so well-built and striking, strong and assured. My eyes delighted in him. He walked with purpose and joy even though he was a slave. I did not understand him. My mind raced when he neared. I wanted him for myself, but he did not want me.

Do not judge me as if you have never desired something you should not have. Do not assume you would never do what I did. Haven't you ever wanted the forbidden or unknown? If your flesh were out of control, would you not chase down whatever it craved so badly? It can happen to anyone who loses sight of all that is around them and focuses only on what they do not have.

Because I was blinded by lust, I did not have the mental clarity to look around and see all that was at my fingertips, my blessings. I lost focus. I could only see Joseph, and my obsession with him drove me. I did not have him yet, but I was determined that he would be mine!

One day when he could not avoid me, I grabbed him, seized him by his cloak and made a direct request: "Come lie with me". At last, nowhere to run or hide and no one to witness our passion. Surely, he would relent. Men always had strong desires for women, and I am a woman of status and means. Surely, he wanted me even more than I wanted him, right? No. As I gripped his cloak, he twisted and ran.

Holding his empty cloak in my hands with no body to embrace, I stood embarrassed and ashamed. But RAGE rang more loudly than my embarrassment. How dare he! In that moment, my blind desire turned into a need for revenge. What if someone saw him running through the courtyard without his cloak? What if someone heard us or saw us? What would I tell my husband?

I had to fix it. How? I had no other choice but to lie and make it appear as if he had made the advances. I hung Joseph's garment for all to see and mocked him for trying to have his way with me. I told them he had tried to seduce me, and I turned him down. That became my story and my truth.

My husband, Potiphar, was enraged. [17] He threw Joseph into prison. I was satisfied with this although I wished he had killed him. I would no longer see Joseph and he would suffer through a miserable life in the dungeon. So be it.

I must confess, though, as days and weeks went by, I often wondered why my husband, "The Chief Butcher," had not ordered this man beheaded immediately. Did he suspect me and my indiscretions? Did he believe this man over me? Did he care about this man more than me? Did my actions speak more loudly than my words? Could he tell I was lying? I toiled with what he knew and what he suspected.

A few years later, I heard of Joseph's restoration to power. He was not coming back to work for my husband, but for Pharaoh. The pharaoh brought Joseph out of the dungeons to interpret his dreams. Pharaoh. The most powerful man I knew had chosen Joseph for such an important task.

Would my shame become known? Would I be divorced or killed for my misdeeds? I am Potiphar's wife. My lack of self-control and lust cost me dearly.

Girls, there is no rest when you are living a lie. Our flesh and our inability or unwillingness to control it can cost us our peace of mind.

For more insight into Potiphar's wife, read Genesis 39.

REAL BATTLES: Getting Out of Our Flesh

We want what we want. So, that means it is sometimes hard to let go of things that bring us immediate pleasure. On a hot day, folks reach for ice cream, cold beverages, umbrellas on a beach, time at the lake and other fun-in-the-sun activities. On a cold day, things like hot chocolate, a warm fire, or a good blanket will bring pleasure. These are all what my grandmother would have called creature comforts. Unfortunately, many of us live our lives looking for the happiness we desire from these creature comforts. We want immediate gratification and to do what feels good in the moment. We want what brings us instant pleasure.

But suppose we flipped mindsets and looked past the immediate to the long term. If I am trying to eat healthier and I reach for ice cream on a hot day, it is hard to stop until it's gone. In the moment, it makes me super happy, and I can easily rationalize it.

"It was only one scoop and it's so hot."

"Nothing wrong with a little ice cream."

Those are great rationalizations; the problem is that ice cream does not help me meet my personal long-term goal.

What I choose to do on the hot day impacts how my future self looks and feels. My choices of today can affect my tomorrows. Provided God grants me more days on this spinning orb of a planet, what I do today impacts what I need to accomplish, how I feel, and how I look tomorrow. We know things happen and everything can change in an instant; it is a truth we have all lived. But, living mindlessly in bad habits and excuses can also change things for the worse. Sometimes, we just need our desires to submit to better habits, healthy mindsets, and God's plans for us.

The word submission has an unbelievably bad reputation. We somehow imagine it means we are owned or enslaved to something. Submission in God's eyes is not weakness or loss of power, entrapment, or thoughtless following. It is the balance of respect and love.

Submission is about bowing to an ultimate authority and doing what is the next right thing. It is about setting aside our will for the will of God in us and through us. It simply means we come into alignment and work together. We have a mission from God and only through submission to His will can we live our best lives for Him and through Him.

If you want real power, tell your flesh to submit to the power of the Holy Spirit in you. When you are guided by the Holy Spirit as your helper, you can live more at peace with your true design.

REAL POWER FOR THE REAL WORLD: I Want, I Think, and I Feel

Let us dive a little deeper into the idea of living out of our flesh versus living out of our spirit. I teach on this in terms of my "I want," "I think," and "I feel." People use these three phrases a lot. Each day, we say or hear someone say, "'I want…, 'I think…' or 'I feel…'" We want, think, and feel multiple times a day.

Sometimes, we want, think, and feel so much that we actually live out of our flesh without realizing it. By constantly fulfilling our desires this way, our flesh rules our days. Our emotions can overrun us incredibly easily when we live this way. If our desires are not fulfilled, we become upset, anxious, frightened, or disappointed and bitter. Our emotions begin taking control of our time and decisions, instead of our spirit. I believe this teaching is an essential understanding for us as women.

We let how we feel about something or someone determine our mood and how we act. Our emotions rule us instead of us having authority and control over them. We have the right to control and harness our emotions. They do not have the right to control and sit in authority over us. There is something to be said for intuition and discernment, but there is also something to be said about living in our spirit more than from our emotions.

What we want is not always the best thing for us. Take this example: If my fictional twenty-year-old son wanted a new car—say, a sports car that tops out at 180 mph. Since he has three tickets on his record for speeding, his desire/want would not be the best choice. Just because he wanted the car, even if he R-E-A-L-L-Y wanted it, does not mean it was the best option for him. Our *"I want"* can be out of balance. It has to be put in check by what God wants for us.

My personal *"I want"* is enormous. I want to be an extravagant giver who lives off of ten percent and gives away ninety percent. I want to help people and situations. I want to develop leaders. I want nice things and amazing memories. I want to be and do what God crafted me for in my mother's womb. I have a lot of wants.

Sometimes, my *"I want"* can sound like it is too much. Sometimes it can sound demanding or rude, like a spoiled child throwing a tantrum. My wants can lead me into competition with others. These are times when my *"I want"* is out of control. Being mindful that, every time I win, someone else loses, helps me balance my *"I want"* better. It is hard to maintain deep, meaningful, life-long relationships if we win every argument and get everything we want.

Our thoughts are powerful. What we think matters, but it can also get in our way. What we think can cause paralysis by analysis. We can overthink and overcomplicate things which makes us exhausted or stuck in making decisions. We can also rationalize things that are dangerous. We can have false narratives. These are things we make up or believe about a situation or person that become our truths.

For example, we might have a hard conversation with someone and then plant ideas daily that they do not like us and are out to get us. In actuality, they may indeed like us but did not like how we handled a given situation, so they had to have a hard conversation with us. Hard conversations are part of life; they do not always mean someone does not like us or wants us out of their lives. False narratives are difficult to realize because they look so real that they appear to be true to us. Beware of lies that look like truths.

We know people can become so intellectually gifted or educated that they block themselves from believing in God or having faith in Him. They may have a false narrative about religion, faith or God Himself. They may have heard only weak or narrow-minded people believe in God. It is a lie the academic world loves to believe and spout. The mind of an intellectual can become their higher power. Even if we do not consider ourselves to be an academic or an intellectual, our *"I think"* can try to outwit God. We may try to argue with Him, open doors He has already closed, or want answers before we obey Him.

Personally, my *"I think"* is the first thing to rise up and want a fight when I don't like a directive or an idea. It can look and sound a lot like arrogance. It interrupts and wants to control. It comes with a harsh tone at times and with questions at other times. I am a thinker and a quick processor, but this attribute can become detrimental if I think before I fully listen to others and to God. Perhaps this is an issue for you. Stop trying to always outthink God and others.

Our feelings are powerful forces. They have the power to hurt and heal. Our feelings change. They will let us down and run us around in circles if they control us. It can be like a dog chasing its own tail. There is lots of barking, growling, and sweating, but nothing is gained. A dog runs and runs but does not actually make any forward progress when it is chasing its own tail. When women feel strongly about something, we can become very frantic and emotional about it. Be careful not to chase your own tail, Girl.

The truth is, our feelings will lie to us and tell us all kinds of things. When we get into our "feelings" about things, we become easily offended. When our feelings are hurt or wounded, we can make up stories in our minds that simply are not true. Our *"I feel"* can lead us into depression, bitterness, blind reaction, rose-colored glasses, and roller coaster emotions.

My *"I feel"* is passionate. I feel things with my whole being, heart, mind and soul. It is the artist in me that *feels* big and very deeply. There are times I am utterly baffled because I do not understand why others don't feel the same way I do about things. This can cause problems if I am not quick to examine the issue from a 360° viewpoint. My angle and view are not the only problems. Following my *"I feel"* can cloud my perspective and cause poor judgment if I don't check it against the Holy Spirit.

My "I want," "I think," and "I feel" will try to find ways to get in the way of my "I Am." If I go into my days and the situations before me and ask the Holy Spirit to guide me, my desires must come into alignment with His. If the Holy Spirit is my guide, then I am living out of my spirit attached to His Holy Spirit—not out of my flesh.

As Christians, we should live by the Spirit. When we become Christ followers, we also get the help of the Holy Spirit to guide us. Are we using Him as much as we should? Are we submitting our will to His will?

Then Moses said to God, "If I come to the people of Israel and say to them,
'The God of your fathers has sent me to you,'
and they ask me, 'What is his name?'
what shall I say to them?" God said to Moses,
"I AM WHO I AM." And he said,
"Say this to the people of Israel:
'I AM has sent me to you.'"
(Exodus 3:13-14)

God is the great I Am and when we let Him rule our days, life and purpose come into balance.

Get Real: Reflection & Prayer

1. How can idle minds and hands lead to questionable choices?

2. How can focusing on what you don't have lead to forgetting who you are or what you do have?

3. When has this occurred in your life and what did it take to resolve it?

4. What can you do to avoid these kinds of traps for yourself?

5. What are your "*I wants*" that get in the way?

6. What are your "*I thinks*" that get in the way?

7. What are your "*I feels*" that get in the way?

Father God,

Please help me to move past myself and what I want, think, and feel, to what You want, think, and feel for me. May I be ever mindful that one idea from You is worth more than a thousand of my ideas. Move me past old patterns and mold me as gently as You can into the women You created me to become.

In Jesus' name,

Amen.

CHAPTER 8

Courage to Fight for the Good and Wisdom to Know What Good Means

*"Fear not, for I am with you; be not dismayed, for I am your God;
I will strengthen you, I will help you, I will uphold you with my
righteous right hand. Behold, all who are incensed against you shall
be put to shame and confounded; those who strive against you shall
be as nothing and shall perish. You shall seek those who contend
with you, but you shall not find them;those who war against you
shall be as nothing at all. For I, the L*ORD* your God, hold your right
hand; it is I who say to you, 'Fear not, I am the one who helps you.'"*
(Isaiah 41:10-13)

REAL LIFE: Some Days It's Hard to Breathe

I had been called out of the audience onto the middle of a stage in a foreign country and asked to sing. Nothing in me wanted to get up and absolutely nothing in me wanted to sing. I had stopped singing for nine months. I couldn't do it, there was no song left in my soul. I am a girl who has been on a platform since age two. Losing my desire to be front and center meant things were not going well in my life.

Through a long series of events, and some incredible friends who wanted to bless me, I found myself in the center of a stage. The room was full of some amazingly talented and fairly well-known people. A former governor and presidential candidate, a two Grammy award-winning musician, an international violinist, and pianist-composer flanked me. It would have been a dream, something I worked for or tried to make happen, had I not been in midst of the deepest grief of my life. Eleven months earlier, I had lost my late husband, Daryl.

I had tried to back out of the trip several times because I did not want to travel. I still could not laugh, smile, or even dream of having a good time. Most days, I did not even want to feel. Numbness and quiet were much more comfortable companions than loud and center stage that day. In so many ways, I did not want to sing and yet, there I was.

When your high-profile friend calls you out, you have a choice to make. He was not trying to pressure me; he knew my pain and knew the road it would take to recover. His wife, my friend, began chanting my name until the audience joined in. I got up and climbed out of the middle seat in the center of the audience. I awkwardly moved through many seats of elderly folks because they had too little room to move. Eventually, I made my way up to the platform, unsure if I would even remember the words.

Thankfully, my dear friend, who was the one that began chanting my name, knew how desperately I needed to be in this place and how much my faith would grow. She had not allowed me to miss the trip. At one point, she threatened to come to my home, pick me up, and fly us both to her house before the trip if I tried to back out. She stood up for my journey through grief when all I wanted to do was wallow in it. She demanded my presence, and I am forever grateful. That night, God placed me within His divine appointment to give me back my joy.

In that split-second when I was finding it hard to breathe and difficult to even function, God had a clever plan. He reminded me how to laugh and my joy began to return. I literally started laughing inside my own mind as I was singing. It was one of those moments when my life did not seem to be my own. It was surreal.

You see, I was standing on a stage in the middle of the Holy Land, Israel. I began laughing, because I was not singing praise songs or hymns, as one might expect in this place. Instead, I was singing *Mustang Sally* at the request of that former governor. I watched the crowd begin to sing along and react to what they were witnessing. Laughter filled my heart and mind.

God's sense of humor caught me off guard that night. He was using my love of music to bring back my joy and wake my sleeping spirit. That stage helped me remember part of my core. I had lost my music, my sense of humor, laughter, and joy. My emotions had all morphed into grief. The audience in front of me had no idea I was a widow. They did not see my pain. They just clapped and sang with me. The audience participation was ridiculously loud. It caused bus drivers and tour guides to come into the room from outside.

As the lyrics were sung, I watched the crowd have so much fun. I began to smile for the first time in months. Then I began laughing and singing all at the same time. I remember thinking, *"This is what it feels like to laugh. I remember this feeling. I like laughing. God, You are funny! Seriously, Mustang Sally in the middle of the Holy Land? I never knew you liked classic rock!"*

When the song was over, the crowd stood as I cried and laughed with tears of joy streaming down my cheeks. I looked around and shook my head. The governor laughed loudly behind me. He knew he had just witnessed God's healing overtake me. On that platform in the middle of Israel, I encountered God in a very unlikely way. I now have lifelong friends I made that night as I turned a corner from the road of grief to the path of healing.

The sorrow may last for the night, but His joy comes in the morning. (Psalm 30:5b) It was "morning" for me; a new dawn. It was time to breathe and learn how to live again. I knew it had been almost a year since I had done either. Do you remember a moment when you smiled or laughed for the first time after a long period of sorrow, sickness, loss, or pain? If you felt guilty about it, that's normal, but it is okay to find your laughter again. Nobody who loved you well would want you to stop laughing forever.

The truth is, God's Word is much more concerned with our joy than our happiness. A form of the word *happy* is used approximately thirty times, but joy is used over three hundred in the Bible.[18] God clearly puts more emphasis on living in His joy. Happiness is an emotion which is often caused by the circumstances that surround us and how we react to them.

With a little research on the website "Quora," we find the root word to "happy" is *ashar* which is Hebrew, meaning "to set right or be blessed".[19] But joy comes as we mature because it has nothing to do with our temporary pleasures. Joy is found in the Lord and **not** based on circumstances. The Greek for joy is *chara*, meaning "to be exceedingly glad".[20]

Paul was a great teacher of gratitude and joy even during his trials. The book of Philippians is a beautiful example of his ability to find joy in the midst of sorrow and suffering. Imprisoned, embattled, shipwrecked, sick, and in chains, Paul still praised God. When we learn how to face trials with perseverance and a focus on Christ, we can find joy much more easily. Gratitude increases joy just as joy should increase gratitude and thanksgiving.

REAL WOMEN FROM SCRIPTURE: PHOEBE

"Bright and radiant." That's what my name means. I am Phoebe. I want those I meet to be well-cared-for and served. My home is open, and my hands and feet move as Christ moved. I am a patron for our church, so I take care of our members in need and offer counsel as I can. Some say it is selfless or sacrificial; all I know is serving others brings me joy.

My homeland sits on the majestic Mediterranean Sea, about nine miles from Corinth. The beauty here in this bustling seaport is almost indescribable. We have the bluest of blues and the greenest of green waters. Our port is busy and bustles with goods and trading. It is here, in Corinth, where I was born and raised. It is also here where I became a follower of Jesus Christ of Nazareth. Then, I opened my home for our church's meeting place. Whatever I have now belongs to us all.

At times, I fear what may become of us because so many others want us stopped and our faith discredited. But the news of Christ lives and breathes in us. Our mission is focused, and our leadership is unshakable, like our beloved brother Paul. This is why I find courage to fight for those among us who are treated with harshness, oppressed and wronged. This act of serving others helps make me stronger. I will not hide or back away.

The life I had before Jesus is nothing compared to what I have now while serving Him. Although, I must admit, there may have been one moment of pause which almost stopped my breath. Our brother Paul asked me to carry his letter to the Romans. It was scary. I was not sure I could do it.

Are you sure, Paul? Am I the messenger you desire to carry such a precious writing to Rome? It is true that I have business of my own there and that many call me "a ministrant of *the Church*". I am a "servant," or *diakonos*—Greek for "deacon" or "deaconess," and understand it matters.[21] But I am still a woman and that also matters in this place. It is my nature to go and to serve. Serving is how I find my joy. Paul, are you sure it is me who should carry the Epistles to the Romans?[22]

Doubt and fear want to play with the anxiety and excuses in my mind. However, my spirit also wants to unite with the Holy Spirit. There is still so much work to be done. Our time is short and the need for the gospel—the truth of Christ—to be shared is greater than my feelings.

Paul assures me that I am intended to take this journey and he will introduce me as part of his letters. Thus, I will be known and trusted because he is known and trusted. I am a sister in Christ,[23] and he has been healed and helped by my hands and my home. There is no need to be anxious or bothered, only a need to be obedient to God's calling. Paul will establish my name in Rome and God will establish my name in history. I am Phoebe.

"I commend to you our sister Phoebe,
a servant of the church at Cenchreae,
that you may welcome her in the Lord in a way worthy of the saints,
and help her in whatever she may need from you,

> *for she has been a patron of many and of myself as well."*
> (Romans 16:1-2)

Girls, don't be afraid when you are assigned an important job. An imposter syndrome is not your truth. Take courage and walk into what God has ordained with your head held high, trusting that He has already gone before you.

REAL BATTLES: Finding a Happy Place

When life is too overwhelming, we may find it hard to smile or walk in peace. We can feel stressed out by our responsibilities at work as well as at home. We may even get dragged down by the weight of what we are carrying, feeling paper thin against the load. God's Word says, "For his anger is but for a moment, and his favor is for a lifetime. Weeping may tarry for the night, but joy comes with the morning." (Psalm 30:5) This is one of my scriptural happy places. It is God's promise that no matter what, the storm will end.

Happiness is based upon circumstances (what is happening around us), but joy comes from the Lord. We can be unhappy and still find joy if we understand the difference. When I think of this, it reminds me of Paul. He was in chains in a prison cell which in no way made him happy, but he still sang praises, told stories of Jesus, and reminds us to count trials as times of joy and growth. No human or thing can ever be your joy giver. That is God's job.

When I need to regroup because life has run me over or I feel entirely inadequate for the tasks at hand, I find His refreshing water. It washes my soul and fills me with fresh energy. Whatever has clogged me up and clouded my walk with anxiety, sadness, or trouble is sifted and cleansed by the ripples and waves. Water is one of my earthly happy places, as are swings, coloring books, my husband's arms, and my tribe. Find your happy place when you need it, Girl, but never mistake it for your joy.

REAL POWER FOR THE REAL WORLD:
Seek Wise Counsel

As women, we tend to turn to our friends, family, and confidants to talk. We talk a lot. We even have conversations with ourselves. We turn to trusted advisors, try to find people who will take our side, and look around us for more advice.

While wise counsel is always good and there are many scriptures attesting to it, it is critical that we make sure our counselors are truly wise. Just because we trust someone does not mean they are the source of wisdom we need in a difficult situation.

So, what are some traits of a wise counselor? Maturity, integrity, discernment, an ability to set aside their own agenda and fear, vision to see multiple sides of an issue, and an earnest relationship with God. Wise counsel will never advise us to do something that would go against God or His Word. They will not just tell us what we want to hear or take our side.

Ultimately, though, God should always have the final word. When we talk to everyone else and seek their advice more than we talk with God and seek His, we are way off course. Learning how to get still and seek God with purposeful prayer and deep roots will benefit us more than the most brilliant Earthly advisor. We will know our roots are growing when the fruit of our lives begins to change.

It is not about fancy words or a formula, it's about coming to Him, being still and learning how to attune so we can listen and grow. Galatians 5:22-23 teaches us the fruit of the spirit, and it is a good way for us to measure our growth in becoming more like Jesus. If we are growing in our love, joy, peace, patience, kindness, goodness, faithfulness, gentleness, and self-control, our roots are getting deeper and we are growing in godliness and wisdom.

I put a word of caution here as a church staff member. Some of my favorite people on this planet are the people I am surrounded with as part of our ministry team. However, we are just people trying to be obedient to our purpose. There are folks who want to see us as the ones with all the answers. We, as church staff members, are all trying to deepen our relationships with Christ too, just like you.

Church staff members and pastors have training and a wealth of resources, and our mission is to help grow the body in the knowledge of Christ. But, those of us who serve on ministry teams are not flawlessly righteous, we are human. Pastors are amazing, but they are not God. Do not worship your church's building or staff, even the pastor, more than you worship the Creator of the Universe. Please encourage and pray for your staff and pastor, they need it. They can be immensely wise counselors, but they are often isolated more than you imagine. Your prayers and support make a difference.

Get Real: Reflection & Prayer

1. What are some things you do to bring laughter into your life?

2. How has God's plan for you been challenging at times?

3. What are some of your happy places and which ones do you need to revisit?

4. When have you felt inadequate for a task or job you've been assigned? How did you make it through it? If you can't think of one, what might you do should you ever face this in the future?

5. Read James 1:2-4. What stands out for you?

6. Think back to situations when you have sought wise counsel. How did you know they were wise?

7. If you could talk to your younger self, what would you tell her about the fruit of the spirit she would need the most? Reflect on the wisdom.

Father God,

May I praise you more. Give me laughter and joy. Help me to become givers of positive power. May my life cause people to stop and wonder what is different about me, because I walk with such contentment and energy. Help me to safely open my home and heart to those in need and those seeking You.

In Jesus' name,

Amen.

CHAPTER 9

Do Prayers Really Matter?

*"Our Father which art in heaven, Hallowed be thy name.
Thy kingdom come, thy will be done in earth, as it is in Heaven.
Give us this day our daily bread.
And forgive us our debts, as we forgive our debtors.
And lead us not into temptation, but deliver us from evil:
For thine is the kingdom, and the power, and the glory, forever. Amen."*
(Matthew 6:9b-13, KJV)

REAL LIFE: Decades of Prayer

Have you ever felt like you were praying to an empty sky? When prayers go unanswered, we can question why we pray in the first place, or how long we should continue to pray. When hard situations arise in everyday life, we may feel like God is not listening or hearing our prayers. If His answers don't come rapidly enough or in ways we understand, we may grow angry or frustrated. Thoughts creep in, like, *maybe He doesn't really care*, or *He has forgotten me.*

God is not a magic genie who requires the right combination of words. We get so hung up on words, but God knows every language on the planet. He needs our hearts to be right more than He needs our words to be exact. Neither is He bound by time frames like we are. He hears and He answers even when we don't like it or see Him working. Does that mean we should stop praying? No, we may be the only person on the planet praying for someone or something. If you are lifting it up to God and standing in the gap, do not let go too early—pray on.

Before I share the story of my thirty-plus year prayer. I want to take a moment to say, this is my story from my perspective. But if you asked them, everyone in my house would have a different perspective. I in no way want to bash my family, nor my stepfather, in particular. We have a good relationship now, but He would be the first to tell you he has learned a lot during his years on Earth. Now he is my Papa, but there was a time when I feared him and hated his actions. But God…

As a young child and teenager, I sought God a lot. In Him I found peace and acceptance. My home life was so chaotic and strained. The alcohol-fueled words I heard there left me deeply damaged and scared. At times things grew violent with more than just words, but most days it was word-filled rage. I knew God from my earliest days, but for several years I was not in church because of everything that happened with my mother and father.

As a teenager, one of my friends asked me to go to church with her and her little sister. I am eternally grateful. I was safe there and found some support. It was a place where I could sing and learn without fear and condemnation. But faith and religion were not easily understood by my stepdad.

One day, he was very angry. In the middle of his explosion, he yelled, "You're some kind of Jesus freak!" He meant it to cause harm, but I wore it proudly. So proudly that I bought a t-shirt with "Jesus Freak" on the front and a cross on the back. He was not good with kids, and he hated himself so much he was convinced that God hated him too. He pushed back, mocked, and rejected everything about faith and church. I would hear him say things like, "God doesn't want me. I have done horrible things" and "I am not good enough for God."

As an adult, I better understood what made him the way he was. He came from a cycle of abuse. His dad was a raging alcoholic who made him drive from bar to bar as a twelve-year-old boy. His assignment was to sit in the car waiting until his daddy staggered out, or was thrown out, then drive him to the next place. Very early in his life, he was beaten and forbidden to see his mom and she was threatened when she tried to see her son. His dad was mean and spiteful.

At some point, his dad dumped him on his grandparents' doorstep and left town for months at a time. My Papa still wasn't allowed to see his mom because his grandparents were afraid their son would find out. This boy who lived close to his own mother was forbidden to know her. They were all trapped by an abusive and controlling man who lived 900-plus miles away before phones were common. Fear enslaves.

One tumultuous evening, my stepdad's father came stumbling through the front door of his parents' home unannounced. He was screaming, slurring his words, and threatening to beat up his own parents if they did not let him take his son back with him to Michigan. My stepdad hid in the corner of a bedroom with a loaded shotgun in his hands.

As soon as his dad opened the bedroom door, my stepdad pulled the trigger. The blast knocked him to the ground, and he dropped the gun. He busted out the window and ran…and ran…and ran. Desperate people do reckless things.

Luckily, he only struck the wall and not his dad, but that day, the man learned his boy was big enough to fight back. My stepdad's anger and bitterness took root and grew. It was fertilized with terror and unquenchable disappointment. Eventually, it would grow so unrestrained it poured out onto everyone and everything in his life.

Researchers say being abused does not mean you will become an abuser, but most abusers were abused themselves at some point.[24] As a teenager, this fact did not matter to me. Living in a cycle of instability was enraging. While my stepdad would only occasionally grow physical, his words cut almost every day. Yelling, screaming, and cussing were just part of the daily routine at my house. My sister Lisa and I used to have a running joke, "If someone doesn't get yelled at or hit or something doesn't get thrown or broken, it's not a holiday."

As an adult, I better understood how to set healthy boundaries, but I was 35 before I learned this was allowed. On my own, I could not bring myself to make these rules and boundaries, but a wise pastor taught me the truth. For example, I would only speak to my stepdad before 4pm, because he would still be sober. I would only stay at gatherings for short periods of time, and attend them during the day, instead of evenings or nights. If he began screaming or threatening, I would leave and not answer the phone for a few days.

I prayed for my Papa to know Jesus for around thirty or forty years. I don't actually remember when I began praying for him in earnest, but I was probably in fourth grade. When I was a third grader, he told me I was the only one in the family that everyone would listen to, and I had to help him keep us together. Why would any grown person seek the help of a small child to hold their marriage and family together? It doesn't make sense to me now, but at the time it seemed about right. My mom threatened to leave and there were five of us in that home, surrounded by drama and trauma all the time.

No doubt others prayed for us, my grandmother for sure. Much of that time, we did not like him or his actions, but my stepdad clothed and fed us. He made sure we had a roof over our heads and by trailer park standards, we had good money with him in our lives. He taught me the importance of keeping my word and how to be observant. These things serve me well and I am grateful for them, but life with him back then was rarely easygoing.

At some point, I knew I had to forgive him, because Jesus forgave me. We forged a relationship as years went on and life mellowed this man. My grandmother had a profound impact on his journey toward faith and my mother's death shocked him. He began to ask questions and to listen. Others played pivotal roles in his understanding of church fellowship, forgiveness, and unconditional love.

He was a survivor, a broken mess, a drinker who no longer found alcohol fun. He was a sinner in desperate need of a savior and God was chasing him down. At age 82, my Papa accepted Christ as his Savior and the Leader of his life. When he called me and said, "I am going to be baptized. Can you be here?" there was nothing I could do but crumble the floor and cry, "Thank You, Jesus, thank You."

I happened to be in a staff meeting with my church team when he called. It was so unusual for my phone to ring at that time of day from him, it compelled me to answer. I dropped to my knees and made him repeat himself. I put my phone on speaker so the team could hear. They cried and rejoiced with me.

My mother had long since passed, and he had been remarried and widowed again. Through everything, he was and is still my Papa. I chose to keep him as a God given part of my life. I will never forget the call or the Sunday I got to see him baptized with his now forever wife. I sat up front, took video, and literally cheered. I am quite sure the people in that little country church thought I was odd, but I just don't care.

When God shows up and shows off like that, there is nothing you can do but praise. Today, this man whom I love does not find great pleasure nor escape in alcohol. His life's perspective has changed. He goes to church every week and is so grateful to be there.

Stay in the game, Girls, and keep praying for those you love. It really does matter.

REAL WOMEN FROM SCRIPTURE: SAMSON'S MOTHER

Perhaps you know a woman like me, and her heartache. Maybe you sat beside her as she wept or perchance you listened to her stories and wept with her. We who are barren, mourn. We are the women who God does not bless with children. Maybe we've had glimpses of hope and then miscarried. We deeply grieve a life lost. We cry out to God, longing to feel the presence of a child in our wombs. Our hearts yearn for this kind of blessing more than many others, yet month after month, year after year, we only have emptiness in our wombs.

I am a hard worker, often found in the daily labors of farming alongside my husband. I'm not unlike many of the world's women, who till the ground, plant the seeds, raise and nurture the crops in order to put food on the table. I try not to complain even on difficult days. This is our way of life and our way of survival. No need to grumble, but there are days when my body aches so deeply, my heart aches even more.

Many times, while on my knees planting, my heart cried out to God for a child. Many may judge me for not having spoken these words aloud.

They do not know my profoundly personal pain nor how many times I have petitioned Him. They do not know how the pain of being barren makes me feel like less of a woman, less of a human, unworthy, and unfit for my husband.

Do those in our town know I have feared my husband would stray and find another woman who can give him children, an heir? How else will his name survive generations? Do they know the intimate prayers I have whispered to God, the bargains I have tried to make? Could they conceive the pleadings of my innermost thoughts and dreams? No, they probably have no idea and they certainly have no right to know my agony. Only God really knows how often I pray these words:

"God, You and You alone are the giver of this miracle. My heart wants what it does not have. Please make the ache and pain go away or give life to my womb. You have heard me for so long, you know my prayer. Teach me how to pray differently if you must, but please answer my cries. God, if You choose not to give me a child, change my heart's desire and I beg you to please help me to accept Your will."

One seemingly normal sunny day, it all changed. As I was going about my routine in the fields, a man of God like an angel appeared to me. He told me I would have a son and gave me very explicit directions regarding what I was to eat and drink. I had to remain clean because my son would be a Nazirite. I felt no fear as I listened, I knew my prayers were being answered. God had heard me in the heavens and was sending a miracle in the form of a baby boy. I ran to tell my husband Manoah.

I told him of the man of God and the explicit instructions on how I was to conduct myself. I told him what I was to eat and drink in order to assure our son was consecrated for his divine purpose of delivering Israel out of the hands of the Philistines. Even though my husband knew my strength and the power of my faith, Manoah instantly began praying that God would allow the messenger to return and teach us.[25] He wanted questions answered and plans laid out. He wanted to hear it for himself.

Would we be so blessed as to take part in parenting a child who would be known in Israel for generations to come? After all this time of trying to have a family to no avail, was Manoah to be selected as the father of an anointed, handpicked, ordained child who would have the favor of God on him from his inception? My husband's spirit was more troubled than mine. He believed, but he wanted to make sure we would conduct ourselves properly even after the birth of this miracle child.

God answered the prayer and allowed the messenger to return, but again I was alone in the field, working and praying over this precious gift to come. I ran quickly to get my husband so he could return with me. The messenger repeated what I had been told and reminded my husband that I was to be careful and obey. Manoah was so pleased, he offered to kill a fatted goat and prepare a feast. The messenger declined to eat and instructed us to make a burnt offering to the Lord. As Manoah went about this sacrifice, the man of God did a most wondrous thing. He leapt into the altar's flame and ascended into Heaven without being burned. He was indeed an angel of God!

After this miraculous sight, Manoah was afraid we would die for having witnessed God Himself. I calmed his mind because my spirit was settled. We would not die, we would LIVE. We would bear a son named Samson who would deliver Israel from its enemies. We would do all we had been told. This is what I knew to be true. God had heard and answered my prayers.

I suppose all mothers believe their children are special, but Samson was crafted by God to be especially unique in many ways. History would note that He would indeed help Israel fight against the Philistines. He became a leader and judge for twenty years. Important work he began would outlive him and not be completed until the armies of Samuel and David finished the tasks. He would be strong and courageous, a Nazarite who tore apart a lion with his bare hands. He knew God's call but was not always the best decision maker, especially when it came to women. As his mother, this situation was devastating. I wanted the best for him, but he made his own choices.

While I loved him and he loved me, I did not always understand him and was often heartbroken over his actions. God had given him, and us, so much. We knew his destiny and the rules that surrounded it. Yet, my heart shattered over his selection for a wife. How could he marry a woman who came from among the very people he was destined, by God Himself, to destroy? When I prayed to conceive, I had no way of knowing how much that baby's choices would someday wound me. Once again, all I could do was drop back onto my knees and pray for my child. It did not matter how old or how grown he was, he was still my child. I would petition Heaven on his behalf now just as I had done before he was conceived.

Mothers in Israel have always been held responsible for the faith of their children. Israelite boys spent their first seven years learning many things from the women of our households. Afterward, they were allowed to go out and work with the men. Had I not taught him wisdom and discernment when he was young? Had I failed my son and God? Was I a horrible mother? Why was he a man who wanted what he wanted more than what we or God wanted for him?

My son let his flesh get in the way of his purpose and we all suffered because of it. I am not the first obedient mother whose heart was crushed by a disobedient child. I am not the only parent who has watched in anguish at their son's choices to only live up to part of his potential. I often wonder how his life and the lives of our people would have been different had he stayed focused on God. I am the wife of Manoah and the mother of Samson, but I am also the chosen daughter of the one true God of Israel. Because of this truth, I still go to the fields and pray. God is real and He hears my prayers.

Girls, she was not the only woman who talked with angels in scripture, but did she know how special this made her? Hannah, Sarah, and later, the Virgin Mary all had these kinds of encounters and received messages from Heaven. Did she know of any similar stories that had come before her, and been passed down through oral teachings? Even if she did, consider the amount of faith it must have taken for her to immediately believe this as her truth and her miracle.

She lived about 12.5 miles from Bethlehem hundreds of years before Jesus was born. Yet in an instant, Samson's mom believed. [26] What a lesson on faith.

For more reading on Samson's mother, go to Judges 13, 14:2-5.

REAL BATTLES: Purposeful Prayers

In full disclosure, I have prayed to become a mother for years and the story of Samson's mother was painful for me to write. As I reflect upon it now, I am not so sure that I did not have an early miscarriage during my first marriage. My late husband and I tried to have children, but after many attempts and years of trying, we found out he had an issue. There was a painful and costly procedure with a fifty percent success rate he could have had done, but we decided it was not worth the risk. We reasoned if God wanted us to have children, we would. It never happened.

To this day, my heart hurts every Mother's Day. Those are Sundays when I don't like being at church. I was not blessed with a baby to call my own. I get that it is a gift from Heaven, and God knows much more than me. But if I am honest, I have also been devastated at times over this unanswered prayer. I have questioned my worthiness or unworthiness and I have heard others question it too—it's hard.

Here is the thing. People often have said stuff like, "You've been a mom to so many kids." While I know this is true, it is not the same. My late husband and I also talked about adoption, but he was not sold on it. If it is not a good choice for both people in the marriage, it should not be pursued. It was not a good choice for him, so it was not a good choice for us. Therefore, I am left childless.

The tears I have cried over not being able to have my own baby are too numerous to count. My heart hurts for everyone who has tried and lost, succeeded then lost a child, and simply wanted but never received. If this is you, you are not alone.

The Bible says children are a gift from God.[27] When I get to Heaven, I would like to understand why some people get the gift and others do not. I hope it will all become clear. God's will and unanswered prayers can be both heavy burdens and big blessings on Earth. This has been one of my burdens. Unfortunately, I have not always carried it gracefully and for that, I apologize. I wish I could have managed my emotions better.

Following my late husband's death, I met amazing widows and listened to their stories. Many had to raise children without fathers. I listened to the painful retelling of how they told their little ones' their "dad" was never coming back home. They told of the gut-wrenching questions from their children about Heaven, where they would live now, and "what-if's" about their mom dying too.

Their struggles and questions were real and raw. Questions about what happened or why God "took" their dads. Questions about who would teach them how to play sports or walk them down the aisle. As those kids grew into teens or transitioned to college, many wrestled anew with grief. I am not sure whose burden is harder, as a widow—those left childless or those being both mom and dad.

I am thankful God's yoke makes it easier for all of us. I am thankful I was a witness and a prayer warrior with women on their knees praying for their children. It moved me outside of myself and gave me a different perspective. At times, we may find it hard to pray or difficult to know exactly what or how to pray. When we are unsure of how to begin, the best place to start is God's Word. It is our roadmap for life. The Bible says God expects us to pray; *"Rejoice always ; pray without ceasing; in everything give thanks: for this is the will of God in Christ Jesus for you"*. (1 Thessalonians 5:16-18, NKJV)

If you are not sure how to pray or it seems overwhelming, consider the steps below.

Ten Steps to Prayer:

Start by asking God to remove distractions while you seek Him.

1. Praise Him.
2. Confess any sin that may stand between you and Him.
3. Ask Him what or who to pray for.
4. Be still and listen; then ask God to bring faces or words to mind. Pray over them.
5. Thank Him for all He has done and all He will do.

6. Intercede for others. I Timothy 2:1 says, *"First of all, then, I urge that supplications, prayers, intercessions, and thanksgivings be made for all people."*

7. Humbly and earnestly ask for the things you need and desire from God. 1 John 5:14 reads, *"This is the confidence we have in approaching God: that if we ask anything according to his will, he hears us."* (NIV)

8. Ask Him — "Anything else, Lord"?

9. Repeat daily. Even if you start with five minutes or less at first, start.

This is not a secret or magic formula; there isn't one. God does, however, give us prayers to follow in the Bible. The Lord's Prayer, for example, is an excellent pattern of how to pray. It is found in Matthew 6:9-13 and Luke 11:2-4. God doesn't need fancy words. He doesn't even need the English language. He just needs you to show up and cry out.

REAL POWER FOR THE REAL WORLD:
Praying Scripture

As Christians, we know that prayer changes things, sometimes instantly and sometimes after long periods of time. Several years after Daryl died, I began to pray another long-term prayer. There are times when you may surprise yourself as life turns and you grow. Not once had I considered remarrying until I realized how alone and lonely I was as a childless widow. I softened to how much I missed being a wife. Things I had never considered before became part of my prayers and my heart's desire.

As my life shifted and my vision changed, I began to ask my tribe of warriors to pray for my husband, whomever he was. I wanted a forever family. It took many years for God to weave our tapestry together. Those long seasons can be challenging as we wait for God's timing instead of our own. All too often, we hear those around us say, "I'll pray for you," but then we wonder if they ever really followed through. Will they actually take the time to pray for us? My tribe did, and oh, how I was blessed.

Prayer should never be a last resort, rather it should be a top priority. It can be an all-day conversation with God or a specific request. But prayer should be ever present on the tips of our tongues. It's not just for professionals, like pastors, preachers, and teachers. God has given all of us this opportunity. It is one of the best ways to grow in our relationship both with Him and with others. It is also an authentic way to support and encourage others.

Prayer and Scripture are two of our weapons. When combined, they are mighty. Praying a scripture purposefully over a situation and even substituting your name or the name of the person you are praying for into the scripture is powerful. It doesn't have to be elaborate to be effective.

Consider this:

> *"But He said to me, 'My grace is sufficient for you,*
> *for my power is made perfect in weakness.'*
> *Therefore, I will boast all the more gladly of my weaknesses,*
> *so that the power of Christ may rest upon me."*
> (2 Corinthians 12:9)

Because of God's promise to all of His children, I can say a personalized prayer such as: *But He said to "Teri", My grace is sufficient for you, for my power is made perfect in your weakness.*

There is something intimate and intense about personalizing a scripture. Consider praying God's Word over yourself, your children, and all those you love.

Get Real: Reflection & Prayer

1. What are your long-term prayers?

2. How has God used and changed your prayer life?

3. When God answers your prayers, do you spend as much time praying thanksgiving as you did for the request? Consider keeping a journal of blessings or answered prayers.

4. What did you learn from the story of Samson's mother?

5. How might her parenting have been impacted by what she knew? Why was she always the one that received more information and revelation?

6. How can you mature your prayer life based upon the steps listed or praying scripture over yourself and those you are petitioning for? Consider writing out a prayer here.

7. Which steps do you do easily, and which ones would you like to be more mindful of as you are deepening your prayer roots?

Father God,

I come in prayer to give sincere thanks to You. Thank You for what appeared to be unanswered prayers, because I know your ways are higher than mine. Help me remember that my views and Your views are very different.

May I again count the blessings for answered prayers I lifted up over years and only thanked You for once. Help me to be Your child with a gracious heart. Let me walk in gratitude daily. Forgive me for not thanking You longer when You blessed me so abundantly. Thy will be done on Earth as it is in Heaven. Thy will be done in me. Thy will, not mine.

In Jesus' name we pray,

Amen.

CHAPTER 10

Powerful Love

*"But if God so clothes the grass of the field,
which today is alive and tomorrow is thrown into the oven,
will he not much more clothe you, O you of little faith?
Therefore do not be anxious, saying, 'What shall we eat?' or
'What shall we drink?' or 'What shall we wear?'
For the Gentiles seek after all these things, and your heavenly Father
knows that you need them all. But seek first the kingdom of God and his
righteousness, And all these things will be added to you."*
(Matthew 6:30-33)

REAL LIFE: I Never Saw it Coming

After many long years of hard work in education, I was blessed enough to start my own consulting firm with a different focus. Now, I do lots of different things. No two days are the same, other than I get to meet and pour into people. I strive to be a life-giving leader who hangs out with world changers and invests in their teams and clients.

A few summers ago, I combined a work trip with a little vacation and headed out on an adventure to some of my bucket list places. The girl from the trailer park was headed over the pond on a grand voyage. I talked a few girlfriends into going with me, because I did not want to take this important trip by myself. Two widows and two divorcees heading to Europe sounds like a joke. While I assure you that none of us ever wanted those descriptors for our lives, they were true. We each have different and yet similar stories including loss and blessings.

We met up at a major U.S. hub and began our escapade of soaking in sights, sounds, long days, good food, grand and hard undertakings, all combined with some work for me. Occasionally, but not daily, I would post a few pictures onto my social media pages. I never want others to feel like I am being arrogant with my travels, but there are things others will only see through those of us who take the journeys. Honestly, most of the time during my travels, I spend less than 24 hours in a city, so I don't really get to see very much.

This was different; it was an intentional pause alongside work with girlfriends I love. If you are single, I highly recommend finding friends who will go on adventures with you. Big and small getaways are good for us. I think Americans spend more time researching and planning vacations and getaways than we do planning for our daily lives. Too often, we let life happen to us and just grind it out. Maybe there is a lesson to be learned there.

After a few weeks away, we began to talk about what we had to do once we got back home. We had an amazing time and knew we would vacation together again someday, but real life was calling. Travelling home led us each to several stops and as we said our goodbyes, we all went in separate directions. As I landed at my local airport, my phone messages began rolling in. To my surprise, the messages were not all about work. One of my travel companions had gotten engaged upon arriving home. Literally,

Powerful Love

John had an engagement ring waiting for my adventurous and spunky friend, Stephanie, when he picked her up from the airport.

We were all still trying to get home and unpacked. Meanwhile, she had sent out this picture of a beautiful ring on her finger. I never saw it coming; not that fast. Nonetheless, I was super excited for her and hopeful for my own prayer of a new forever family. Stephanie was a fellow widow who had experienced a beautiful first marriage which ended in a tragic tale. This new beginning was her God surprise. I wish I could tell you the entire story of how He brought them together. It is one of those stories that gives you evidence that God sees us, but it is her story to share in her own book someday, not mine.

A few days after I got settled back in from our European adventure, I had some headshots done for our new church staff pictures. When I posted one of them as a new profile picture on social media, I saw a comment that caught my attention. It said, "I see you." It was from an acquaintance, a widower named Bryan, who rarely commented or posted on anything. It was out of character for him. It took me by surprise, but it also made my heart skip a beat.

Even though I didn't know him well, I knew our grief journeys were actually similar in some ways. He had loved and lost his wife Gina, who had been diagnosed with breast cancer. While undergoing treatments and seemingly doing well, she suffered a heart attack in their home one Tuesday night. Bryan's military training kicked in, as he placed her on the floor and performed CPR until the ambulance arrived. Tragically, she passed eight days later, having never regained consciousness. Bryan and I had met once, just a few months after her passing.

He came into town to perform part of a military retirement ceremony for a mutual friend. The friend's wife wanted to introduce us. She asked if I could help him through his grief journey because I was further along the path. He was only about nine months out of Gina's death, but had set it aside as best he could to be there for his friend. He tried to hide it, but if you know what you are looking at, it is as clear as a sheer rain poncho.

He was heavy with grief and trauma. We began a kindred friendship and over the years since that meeting, we had messaged occasionally. The Holy Spirit would press me to pray for him at times, and I would touch base to make sure he was doing okay.

I have heard it said numerous times, God brings people into our lives for a reason, a season, or a lifetime. I thought this one was just a season turned into a lifetime, and I never saw it coming. God redeems and restores in so many ways. Even though my tribe and I had been faithfully praying for years that God would send me a forever family, I had no idea I already knew him, just like Stephanie had no idea she would come home from vacation to a beautiful ring.

Why should we be so blessed as to have love again? Only God knows.

REAL WOMEN FROM SCRIPTURE: WOMAN AT THE WELL

My days have so many regrets attached to them. Men have passed me around until I feel used up and unworthy. I feel like filthy rags with holes and bare threads still trying to do their work until they are tossed aside with the garbage and forgotten. I have known so many things of this world; anger, hate, loss, regret, enslavement, betrayal, labor, fear and numbness. Numbness is closest to death.

I am trapped in my sin, desperate for a different life, and maybe a new city. There must be something more than this, but there is no fresh start for a woman like me. I have been married five or six times. Why bother counting anymore? For that matter, why bother getting married anymore? I am shunned my own villagers and people will not talk to me. Even women turn from me. I feel less valuable than a camel or an ox.

My shame hangs on me like an old, worn out, dirty cloak trying to mimic a fitted dress. Shame hugs me so tightly I can barely breathe, but everyone sees my stains. I am adorned with disappointment, doubt, worry, pressure, and survival. Have you ever had days when you were just trying to survive? This is how I live the days of my life. I am hated. I cannot even be around other servant women. I am an outcast. No one sees me and if they do, it rarely ends well.

My days all run together. Today is just another, occupied by hard work and thankless living. I must carry heavy jars to fetch water. Fetch, haul, clean, cook, try to do something right. Repeat. It is my daily routine. I cannot haul water during the cool of the morning, and chat with the other women. I must wait until I can slip in and out of the village without being seen.

It is hot here in the desert and the days are long. The noon day sun blazes through the clouds and roasts my skin. It is relentless, but I must go to the well anyway. I pick up my carrying stick and gently place a clay water jug onto each end. They are light now, but the weight of the water will press down on me like the burden of my life once these jugs are full. Every step will be measured by the weight against my balance.

As I approach the well of our revered forefather, Jacob, I notice a man. What is he doing at the well, especially at this time of day? He is obviously a Jew. He must be lost; they would never come here by choice. Jews travel out of their way to avoid setting their feet onto Samarian soil. Our nations have fought for so long, we cannot possibly find peace now.[28] I want to turn and run, but I need the water. I will remain quiet, conduct my business and move on. Surely, he will not try to talk to me anyway.

I approach, set down my jars, and begin the process of drawing up water. Then, He speaks. Isn't this against the rules? Aren't Jewish men forbidden to speak to women? Especially Samaritan women? Am I not an outcast by race, by gender, by class? I look around. Is He speaking to me? He was. He saw me and asked for water. Why would He risk being seen in conversation with me?

Through one question and the short conversation that followed, my life was given new meaning. At the well, my ordinary day changed into an extraordinary day. My sin-filled life was given new hope with a fresh start.

It was a day I would never forget.

That day forever changed my life and the lives of my village. It was the day a Jewish man saw right through the soul of a Samaritan woman.

His people despised me because of my race. My people despised me because of my sin. He did not care, His ministry was for me too.[29] But this man, the living Son of God, He is the Messiah. He told me so Himself…what an honor. He saw me and knew my sin; yet He told me how to find eternal life and living water.

It was my redemption day. He sought contact with me before I even knew of my need for His existence. He gave me a clear picture of His divinity and I could not hide it. My joy overflowed. Because of my story, many in my town came to know Christ. The people of my village could see my change immediately and heard my tale of this man. They ran to Him and asked Him to stay among us. He gave us true life, healing, freedom, and eternity. It was no ordinary day at the well, and my burdens are no longer heavy.

I never saw it coming.

Girls, what is it in your life or spirit that needs the refreshing flow of living water? Go to His well and seek no more.

For more on the woman at the well or the Samaritan woman, read John Chapter 4.

REAL BATTLES: Grown Ups Have Baggage

By the time we reach adulthood, we all have baggage of some kind. We have made mistakes or choices we wish we could take back. They may be represented by small handbags or big trunks full of regret and wrongs, but we all have baggage. There is no way around it. We are not perfect. Our words, our actions, our lives, our families, our workplaces are not perfect.

While we should be willing to help and care for others, we must be careful about picking up others' baggage. This is hard for those of us who are helpers, servants, and fixers. Hear the cautionary tale. Take it in, and learn this lesson from reading, studying, and praying. Learn it before someone else's baggage weighs you down, trips you up, or makes you fall flat on your face.

As women, our friends and loved ones come to us for advice. If we are helpers, servants, and fixers, we try to solve their problems for them. It may be an easy solve by just talking it out, but all too frequently we pick up their baggage and carry it ourselves. We take ownership of their problems and create solutions, or temporary fixes. It makes us feel smart and needed. When we do this, they may come back to us time and again to fix things and give them solutions. What if we taught them how to find their own solutions and be confident in them?

We make great plans, hand them out, and send people on their way. Usually, we become extremely frustrated because they don't follow through on our advice. Understand that people are not you. Most of the time, they will not do what you would do. Understand too, that some people do not want their problems fixed. They just want you to carry their burdens, so they don't have to. Others enjoy being surrounded by drama and fixing their problems would leave them bored.

Sometimes a loved one's baggage becomes so heavy, we cry or scream over it. Just like each snowflake is unique, each tear is unique. God sees us and knows our tears. It is a scientific fact, that each tear and its chemical makeup is unique. Under a microscope, the cause of the tear can be determined. Happy or sad can be seen in the construct of the chemical makeup itself. [30] It's a beautifully designed fact that somehow comforts me. God knows how much we cry. He sees our tears.

> *"You keep track of all my sorrows.*
> *You have collected all my tears in your bottle.*
> *You have recorded each one in your book."*
> (Psalm 56:8 NLT)

It is okay to cry for those we love and help them. But we must also be okay with leaving the burdens and baggage at the foot of the cross with Jesus. He is the only one with enough power, strength and wisdom to solve a problem permanently.

REAL POWER FOR THE REAL WORLD:
Train for the Battles

The world can blindside us with unexpected gifts and unexpected tragedies. When we are blindsided, we spin out of control. What should you do while you are spinning? Make it stop. Stand still. Take a breath. If standing doesn't work, get on your knees. There is something about our body falling to our knees that's powerful for our spirits.

Don't forget what you know. Athletes, military members, and first responders say things like: "Rely on your training." That means we have to train for the world. We must learn about conflict resolution, problems solving skills, controlling our blood pressure and stress levels. We must train for what comes at us. The enemy launches hand grenades at us every day trying to blow us up and move us off our path. Other people's irresponsibility can become our problem to navigate. Choices we make can go wrong and we must correct and not crumble.

Train by memorizing Scripture you can call out in hard moments. Be ready to call on the Holy Spirit to help you make quick course changes and corrections. Train by developing discipline with prayer and study. Train by fasting and seeking with your whole heart.

Training is only made complete through time with God. He is our power source. When life happens, don't forget what you know and Who you know. Armor up.

"Finally, be strong in the Lord and in the strength of his might. Put on the whole armor of God, that you may be able to stand against the schemes of the devil. For we do not wrestle against flesh and blood, but against the rulers, against the authorities, against the cosmic powers over this present darkness, against the spiritual forces of evil in the heavenly places."
(Ephesians 6:10-12)

Get Real: Reflection & Prayer

1. Describe times when you have been unexpectedly blessed.

2. How has God taken you on unexpected adventures that were difficult but necessary?

3. What tools or people do you use when you are faced with difficult situations you did not see coming?

4. What did you learn from the story of the Samaritan woman at the well?

5. What are actions you can take to make other women feel less like outcasts?

6. Write out the full armor of God from Ephesians 6:13-20. Reflect upon what each piece of the armor does for a mature Christian.

7. With question six in mind, which pieces of armor are sturdy, and which need a makeover in your wardrobe?

Father God,

Thank you for always seeing me, even when I feel undeserving and unwelcomed. Put opportunities in me path for me to serve others who may feel the same way. As I serve, help me to learn how to love others and myself more.

May there never be a day when I cast others aside because they are different than me. May I always strive to act and look more like Jesus.

In His name and by His authority, I pray,

Amen.

CHAPTER 11

Chasing Down Hope

*"Peace I leave with you; my peace I give to you.
Not as the world gives do I give to you.
Let not your hearts be troubled, neither let them be afraid."*
(John 14:27)

REAL LIFE: Discontented Days

"Be still and know that I am God."
(Psalm 46:10)

"And we know that for those who love God all things work together for the good, for those who are called according to his purpose."
(Romans 8:28)

Does anyone have trouble with these verses beside me? Being still is not one of my favorite things, unless I am by the water. I am not a fan of being still or quiet on a normal day. And in the middle of a problem, my first thought is not, *"This is good."* I know God will work things out but, I am a work in progress on stillness. For me, these times and verses are not always easy.

Learning how to be at peace and being content is a daily chore. I often want more than what I see. I want more joy, more influence, more funds, more ministry opportunities, more time, more legacy impact. I want more, and yet I am blessed with so much. Walking in gratitude has become intentional for me. Intentional gratitude does not mean that I do not dream of more. I have fewer years on this planet than ever before, so there is an urgency for me.

Before I reconnected with Bryan, my forever husband, I had become discontent with life as a single. I was blessed once with what most people search a lifetime for and never get - a wonderful loved-filled marriage. I grappled with deserving it, but I knew I wanted more. I figured God would provide the man if He wanted me to remarry.

For years, my friend Erika and I had a running joke. God would need to wrap a big bow around a man and drop him on our doorsteps, if he were the guy we were supposed to marry. We both had bad dating experiences and did not really trust our choices. She and I wanted nothing less than God's best for us, and we were willing to wait. Waiting is hard and lonely. If you are still single, hang in and know God will work out His absolute best plan for you in His timing.

I am not sure married people realize how difficult and isolating being single in America can be. We are a couples' society and when you are single, you often experience the "odd man out" feeling. Ever sat next to the empty chair at the restaurant or dinner table? Ever went to the movies, a concert, or the holiday party by yourself? They can be lonely adventures.

As Bryan and I began talking more, I realized he was in the same emotional space. He was ready to date, and he wanted a life partner.

We knew a relationship between us was going to be difficult at best. I was never good at dating and don't really find the sport in it. It's like a bad fishing tournament in my mind. You wait for a pretty day, throw a line out, hope something bites, and pray you don't have to throw it back in for being over or under weight, the wrong type, or dangerous. I know it's odd, but this is my assessment.

However, with Bryan, it was no ordinary date. He lived 900-plus miles away from me, had avoided talking to me for years, and had to hop a plane to have dinner. When he asked, "Would you like to go on a proper date with me?" I had no idea how that would work. Certainly, he could not fly all day just for a four-hour adventure. Instead, he rented a room at a local hotel and flew in for a weekend. Basically, I had 72 hours to get to know someone and decide if we were to remain friends or become possibilities.

Within the first few hours of that weekend, most people would have been done. He rented a room that literally smelled like a dead rat had been in it. You know that strong, you cannot explain away the stench smell? The kind of smell that lingers in your nostrils hours after you have left or destroyed it. It was that kind of bad. It was a smell that makes you think medicinal old folks' muscle ointments would be a great odor alternative. We got his money back and went off to find another hotel.

By the time we got back to my place for our first dinner, there was a HUGE problem. I had left dinner in the oven and the bowls had melted. No exaggeration, there were flames in the oven. We opened the oven door, threw in flour, slammed the door fast and prayed. Within the first three hours, we had been to two hotels and saved a three-story house from a basement apartment fire. I could not do anything but laugh as he stood with open doors and windows, holding up a fan to blow the smoke out of my apartment after the fire stopped.

Needless to say, "date" number one ended in Mexican food and a lot of memories. It was months later before he found out that I am actually a really good cook. Yet, somehow, by day two of the marathon weekend, he was hooked. I, on the other hand, was running. Girls, when God gives you a man who earnestly seeks the will of Heaven for his life plan, nothing will stop it, not even you.

Though life had crushed both of us, in many ways, we still had hope. God's purpose for our meeting so many years ago and His power in our lives was evident and real. You never know who He will allow you to meet. One divine appointment at a retirement ceremony was leading to the possibility of a whole new life.

While it would take Bryan and I some time to learn how to fully trust each other in today's world, we had individually put our trust in Jesus Christ many years before. Because of that, we knew His best would be the absolute best for each of us, even if there had never have been a date number two.

Girls, I promise, one encounter set up by the hand of God changes everything. Just like one encounter with Jesus changed everything for so many women scattered throughout the Bible.

REAL WOMEN FROM SCRIPTURE: WOMAN WITH THE ISSUE OF BLOOD

I have lived with this condition for so long, some days I think I will have to live with it forever. I have tried doctor after doctor for twelve years. It is always the same routine. Find a doctor and tell them my entire history.

When did it start?

What happened?

What have you tried?

Would you be willing to…?

Nothing worked. Nothing. I am weak and worn. I am sick and tired of being sick and tired. I cannot be content with living like this anymore. I have to try. I know it's crazy, but I must try.

You have no idea how desperate I am. Imagine living as an "unclean" for twelve years. I cannot be close to others. I cannot be touched by anyone. I cannot touch other peoples' things. I am a walking dead person.

The laundry and washing are unbearable. I am so disgusted and exhausted by the constant washing just to try and keep my clothes clean. Blood stains everything I own. Loneliness stains my heart. Isolation stains my life. Tears stain my face. But blood, it stains it all.

Jesus is nearby today. I have heard of His miracles. They say He heals the sick, the lame, and the blind. I must go to Him. He is my only hope. I am out of money, out of doctors, and quickly running out of time. I don't care what could go wrong today, because I believe too much in what could go right.

Jesus heals. He is the Messiah; I just know it. If I can get to Him, He can heal me. I have faith. I have hope. I have wild courage. I will cover up as much as I can so I can press in close without being recognized.

The crowd is loud, and the sun beats down on all of us. It is so hot today. The pace is fast; I am quick-stepping to get through the crowd and to get closer to Him. I hear Jesus has been summoned to the home of one of the synagogue leaders. This man's daughter is dying.

I can't go to synagogue. I am unclean…

I miss worship.

I am determined, but also a bit frightened. My heart is beating rapidly. Should I even try to stop Jesus as He goes to the bedside of a dying girl? Oh, my goodness, there He is! It's Him, I… I ….

Maybe if I just reach out…

    And …

        Touch…

            The…

                Hem …

                    Of …

                        His …

                            Garment?

Praise God! Praise God. It STOPPED! PRAISE GOD!

Oh no, He has stopped too. Immediately, He knew someone had touched Him in faith. I did not. I did not touch Him, I just touched His cloak, but I did touch it in full faith that even this small brush with His pure divinity would heal me.

I believe, Jesus, I believe! No matter what happens next, I believe.

He did what the others could not. In that moment, I knew the difference between divine intervention, God's best for me, and what man could not do. At once, I was given peace and completeness. There would be no more poking and prodding, no more questions with condemnation behind them.

Jesus, Jesus, thank You, Jesus!

I will just stay here crying, shaking, and praising You. He turns. He looks over the sea of faces. So many people pressing in close to Him vying for attention. *"Someone touched me, for I perceive that power has gone out from me."* (Luke 8:46b) Oh my, He wants to know who touched Him.

What do I do? I am frightened and trembling, but I must let Him know it was me and go forward. As I move and know that I am healed, I am overwhelmed. I fall before His feet to confess. I am the one who touched your garment, and I am healed. Let all who can hear know my truth. I AM HEALED.

My heart raced not knowing what to expect next. Then simultaneously, the greatest love I had ever known was given to me. Jesus called me "Daughter" and told me my healing occurred because of my faith. He told me to go in peace.[31] In the middle of a crowded desert street, my life was forever changed because I had faith enough to grab hold of His Divinity.

Girls, how about you? What do you need to take hold of through Jesus? Do you need healing from the touch of His garment? Do you need the world to know your story of truth given through Him?

To read more on the beautifully powerful story of the Woman with the Issue of Blood, see Matthew 9:20-22; Mark 5:25-34; Luke 8:43-48.

REAL BATTLES: Chronic Illness

My sister Lisa lived thirty years longer than they said she would. She was sick almost all of her life, but she rarely complained about it. She struggled with literal life and death choices more often than I can count.

I remember being in eighth grade when we went to the hospital with her the first time for some serious medical issues.

She had a stroke and they found out she was born with nothing on the right side, no ovary, no kidney, no appendix. Her other kidney was malformed and minimally functioning and she was a diabetic. BAM! In one day, everything changed for her and for us.

We had always known she was sickly, anemic, and little. She weighed 98 pounds or less when she graduated high school, which is pretty much what I weighed by third grade. She was tiny, but she was also one of my superheroes. They told her at age eighteen that she had five years to live. She did not accept their expectation as her own.

Lisa and my oldest sister, Roni, who is in the medical field, set out on a decades-long journey to give Lisa a fighting chance and new ways to live. We used to joke that she had nine lives, because she "cheated" death so many times. After coming out of comas or serious medical incidents, she would describe what some call near-death experiences like watching her doctors work on her from "above" the table or visiting our mom and my late husband in Heaven.

I am not sure where you land on these kinds of near-death experiences, but Lisa believed she had them and would describe them with intricate detail. Her conditions and symptoms often baffled her medical teams. She had to move away from Arkansas. After being one of the first kidney transplant recipients in the state, she moved to Houston. She found a new medical team with more advanced training, more trials, and more experience.

She took meds she paid for out-of-pocket costing over $1,500 a month just so she could stay alive. I watched her and my oldest sister diagnose her when specialists gave up. I watched her fire doctors and hire other ones from her hospital bed. I watched her run her own business and keep working even when she was ill.

Lisa was a force and, at times, a bit hot-headed. Yet, in general, she was shy. She was always watching and observing, rarely speaking first. She learned how to listen and make people laugh. She was a quick problem solver but utterly ditzy somedays. Her life was more black-and-white or navy and gray than colorful. She played her full hand and never took a day for granted. What I learned from watching Lisa live was how to die with dignity and choice.

After surviving numerous strokes, diabetes for thirty-plus years, open heart surgery, pain, relentless itching I cannot even describe, and hard choices, she grew weary of it all. Her transplanted kidney was dying, and she was back on peritoneal dialysis. The road ahead to a new kidney appeared long and more difficult than the mountains she had already climbed.

She talked with us all and made her choice. We were back in the hospital when she began to question her Houston medical team about stopping all treatments. I watched her nephrologist stand in stunned silence with a tear running down her face. Normally a composed medical professional, she broke. Her endocrinologist, whom she had been with for years, stepped into the hallway to regain her composure. It was a heavy day, but my sister gathered all the information she needed to face her death.

Lisa managed an unbelievably complex life with a ton of humor, and a good bit of occasional cursing. I have stories about my sister that would make you pee yourself just a little, but she was private in many ways, so I'll leave them be. Lisa struggled with life choices. She did things that hurt God's heart, and she battled "why" at times. She was an unperfect control freak.

Above all else, she would want you to know that she LOVED Jesus! Lisa struggled with identity and who she loved on this planet, but once she realized Jesus loved her anyway, her life shifted. When she grabbed hold of the fact that through Christ, she was flawless, she made choices to help get everyone in our family into Heaven. She wanted our sisters, nieces, and their children to surrender to Christ as Lord. She would say, "We have to get everyone's duck in the same pond." The pond was eternity and Lisa had an urgency for our family to be there with her.

As her kidney transplant began to fail and her body struggled with so many issues, Lisa made a choice to go into hospice. Years before, my sister Lori had selflessly given one of her kidneys to Lisa. We both scrambled to get to the hospice location from our home states in time to say goodbye. Meanwhile, Lisa and Roni checked into the hospice facility and had some final and intensely difficult conversations about was acceptable and necessary in that place.

I am forever grateful Roni walked this hard road with Lisa because I could not have done it. I made it in time to talk with my favorite person on her last day. Lisa was still coherent when I arrived. We shared a few words and giggled a few more times before she went back to sleep. Lori made it in time to say goodbye, too. God gifted us those few precious moments.

The night was long. Death did not come too quickly. Lisa was in and out, then she just began to sleep. Her breathing was heavy, but she was resting. I took watch so Lori and Roni could sleep. What happened next may change everything if you are on the fence about faith. I was writing in my journal while I watched and listened to everyone sleep. I heard Lisa begin to move her arms and legs around a bit, so I stopped writing and watched her.

As clearly as you are reading this paragraph, I heard her say, "Jesus, can I come home now?" I smiled and kept watching. She murmured and then got silent, as if she was listening. Then, all of a sudden, she said, "Yes, Sir!". A few hours later, I was taking a nap and Roni was on duty. I awoke to Roni patting Lisa's hand and saying, "It's okay, Sister, go on home now." It was time…. how could it possibly be time?

I was a little over three years out of my late husband Daryl's death—in my arms. I knew I could not watch her take her last breath. She was my person. Why…. now what? The trauma was too much. I picked up the Bible and read Lisa's favorite scriptures in Psalms out loud, from the corner of the room. Lori woke up. She was exhausted from her long drive and had been sleeping hard. A few minutes later, we watched as Roni patted Lisa's hand and ushered her into Heaven.

That night, I watched my sister touch the hem of Jesus' garment and go home. Her faith had brought her healing, it just happened to be on the other side of this life. She was my go-to person and my heart ached immediately. Yet, I rejoiced that hers was whole and full for the first time in a very, very, long time. She had held hope closely for as long as she could and was finally and completely healthy …no more pain. Praise be to God.

REAL POWER FOR THE REAL WORLD:
More Than Just A …

Hope is our superpower when the world gets a complicated kind of real. If we let go of or lose hope, we will fail. We have all heard stories of survivors of horrific disasters making it out against all odds. We have heard of people living through being trapped under ground or rubble for days or weeks. We have seen news stories of people who have survived at sea or in the mountains when they should not have made it out alive.

Why?

Hope and prayer.

So many survivors point to these two things. As long as we hold on to our hope, we can keep going. Don't give up, don't give in, ever.

You are just a Girl…with the strongest Father ever. No contest. Case closed. He wins.

You are just a young lady…with a Father who has the biggest plans for your life; more than you can imagine.

You are just a woman…with a sword and a shield. Laden with a coat of arms from the Creator of the Universe. War on, Princess.

Don't believe the enemies of your mind or of darkness. Do not believe their "just a" for you. Have faith in the fact that you were created for a purpose. It's your gift from God and your truth for all your days.

Get Real: Reflection & Prayer

1. How do you manage stillness and waiting?

2. What is an area of discontentment for you? What about that area might you need to turn over to God?

3. Describe a time when you had bold or unwavering faith.

4. What did you learn or find interesting about the Woman with the Issue of Blood?

5. How has chronic illness impacted your life or the life of someone you know? What is the hardest part of long-term health issues?

6. Write out two scriptures you find hope in for healing or health?

7. What do you need to remain hopeful about in today's society?

Father God,

Help me to grab hold of how much You love me and how the blood of Christ makes me flawless before You. When I suffer from the world's drama, trauma, poor choices, health issues, and stress, help me to hold onto hope and know that You are right here with me.

May I be a real Girl who walks in Your power and not my own. When I struggle with loving or trusting You enough, draw me closer. Capture my heart, mind, and spirit. Let me surrender to You. Give me complete healing and hope.

In Jesus' name,

Amen.

CHAPTER 12

Choose Kind Words

"Get rid of all bitterness, rage, anger, harsh words, and slander, as well as all types of evil behavior. Instead, be kind to each other, tenderhearted, forgiving one another, just as God through Christ has forgiven you."
(Ephesians 4:31-32, NLT)

REAL LIFE: Fighting Fair

As the youngest of four girls, and the youngest of eight kids (counting step-siblings), I grew up knowing how to fight for myself or hide really well. By nature, I am not a fighter. I prefer to talk things out or leave. I ashamedly admit to hiding in a phone booth once in my early thirties. My oldest sister and I were taking care of our sister Lisa at the hospital one night when a bunch of Lisa's friends showed up a slight bit inebriated. My oldest sister, Roni, was not having it.

She politely explained that Lisa needed to rest and asked them all to leave. They declined. From there, it did not go well. Roni gave them a few minutes and then told them to go ahead and pack up. As things continued to get tense, Roni stood up. I knew what would happen next because I had lived with her for years. Those people were leaving; they just did not fully understand that yet.

I silently slipped out the door of the room, went around the corner to an old-school phone booth, and ducked into it. There was no phone, so there was plenty of room. The bottom half of the door had a white film over it, so you could not see through it. Awkwardly, I bent down onto the floor and stayed covered. It's an embarrassing story, but true.

In all fairness, I could still hear everything and if it came to blows, I surely would have bolted to the rescue. (These are the stories we tell ourselves.) Do not worry, I have apologized to Roni several times over the years for leaving her by herself. However, I assure you she is more than capable of fully managing any situation if the need arises. After years working in surgery and post-op, with patients doing all kinds of drugged, incoherent, and crazy things, she can restrain pretty much anyone, as needed.

Wouldn't it be nice if all fights were this easy to see coming? Unfortunately, they are not. In our workplaces, extended families, marriages, and close relationships, fights may have been brewing for months or years before they erupt to the surface. Then they explode with such volatility, the damage left behind takes enormous effort to clean up and repair.

In the current day and age, we also have a new way to fight — by hiding behind a screen. There are some users who go so far as to hide behind fake names on their social media accounts. Anonymity provides them even more freedom to blast people with whatever they choose to say. There is little-to-no accountability for this kind of language, abuse, or fight. If we do not even know who is doing the fighting, how are we supposed to cover and protect, or fight fairly?

When did it become okay for grown adults to hastily spew filth, lies, and insults out of our mouths and call it truth? When did we decide it is okay for us to berate someone for not having the same beliefs as us? Do we honestly think these actions are pleasing to God? When I was a kid, a bully was someone who beat kids up on the playground or right off the edge of campus. Now, they are all over the news and social media.

We have forgotten how to fight fair with those who have opposing views. Children are scolded all the time about what they say and what they post on social media, but who is scolding the grown-ups? In the heat of the moment, it is hard to fight fair. When our minds and tongues have gone into fight mode, we carelessly sling incendiary words and volatile actions around. We do not take time to think of the aftermath when we are trying to wound people or win a fight.

The problem with these kinds of fights is that they also leave us with broken and damaged relationships. This leads to unfriending people virtually and in real life because of our words and rash choices. It can take a lifetime to build meaningful relationships and minutes or a meme to destroy them. Rebuilding trust once it has been shattered can take years.

Fighting fair is not about staying clear of hot topics. Rather, it is about staying on topic, listening, and not letting things get personal. It is also about being willing to examine different viewpoints and not getting too emotional about anything. When we let our emotions override our reasoning, we escalate to straight up ugly and inappropriate places. Letting ourselves go to ugly—in the middle of a fight—will leave us with regrets.

How can we avoid this behavioral trap?

- Be intentional when choosing our words.
- Stay on topic and avoid bringing up painful issues from the past.
- Pause or take a break when things become overheated. Ask for a time when you can come back together in a few hours or days. If there is no time to stop the conversation, use the tried-and-true method of counting to ten before speaking.

When you hear or feel things getting too emotional, call a time out, go to the restroom, or ask for a water break. Stepping away from the table for a few minutes can help emotions calm and conversation to be more productive.

We do not have to agree with everything someone says or does to be kind to them. We do not have to like their choices to show compassion. Kindness goes a long way in building healthy relationships. However, having a way out of a conversation that starts to turn negative is a helpful tool.

When I am training executives and ministry teams for hard conversations or teachers on classroom management, I tell them to have their taglines out. These are sentences that you have practiced so much that they come to you naturally. Your brain does not have to think about them.

Taglines buy your brain enough time to pause and regroup. When I have a hard conversation and I do not agree with the other point of view, I will say, "That's interesting," or, "Can we look at this from a different perspective?" This gives me time to pause and allows the other person space to rethink. It also helps me to find kind words instead of saying unkind or unhelpful things.

When all else fails, remember that forgiveness is both real and powerful. Use it, because there will come a day when you need someone to offer it to you. Once you have forgiven someone, do not hold on to past wrongs. Let them go. It is okay to have healthy boundaries, but it is not okay to keep score of wrongs. Grace should usher us into fair fights and peaceful resolutions.

REAL WOMEN FROM SCRIPTURE: JOB'S WIFE

We have all had those moments we wish we could get back. The moments when we let our feelings and soul overtake our spirits. Days when what we want, think, and feel get in the way of what God has for us. These are times when the pressures of the world overwhelm us, and we just do not think we can do it anymore.

When we are this far under, we cannot play the games or pretend to be happy for one more hour. We cannot understand, believe, or find the desire to face another day in the turmoil. When life's circumstances have shaken us to our core, we just want to shut down. Those kinds of days make us want to stay in our beds, eat, take naps, and start over tomorrow.

Now imagine if you had this kind of day—the worst day of your life—and it was recorded for everyone to see and hear. None of us would want our legacy to be seen in this light. None of us would want our personal or family tragedy displayed for everyone to comment upon. Unfortunately, it is my fate. I am Job's wife. Everyone knows about the day of my greatest sin and shame.

I thought it could never happen to us, but my family and I were caught in the vortex of an epic battle. I could not fathom all that was occurring, yet horribly bad scenes were playing out before my eyes.

Hadn't I been a loving wife and mother whose home was filled with the finer things of life? Yes, I knew I had been. Our family had prospered, and I had been part of its pulse. Laughter and abundance had been our friends, but then one day it was all but stolen from us.

I did not understand. We had been blessed by God and my husband had been a pillar of our community. I had been a proud supporter of him and all ten of our children until the day of the incidents. That was when it all changed. It was the day we spiraled onto the edge of the pit of hell itself. Our lives were turned upside down and we were never the same again. Tragedy upon tragedy struck us.

Sadly, I broke under the weight of grief and dishevelment. Please try to understand where I found myself. Living in abundance and wealth, loving my family, and taking care of our children had been my blessing and joy. In less than 24 hours, everything we had worked for and known was gone.

E-V-E-R-Y-T-H-I-N-G!

One beautiful day, the fury of evil was unleashed upon us. I understand that dramatic and unexpected losses are never easy, but the harshness and sacrifice were more than I could bear in such a short time. Within a matter of minutes, three servants rushed to my husband one afternoon to tell him all our livestock had been stolen or lost in a great fire. These men all came from different locations. How could such calamity be coming from multiple places at once? They told of invading mobs, bandits, and a fire that took not only our livestock but the lives of our servants. Our wealth was gone.

If these were the only disasters we faced, perhaps I would not have broken. Job, in his wisdom, could have made more money. We could have recovered our footing. But the worst news of all was moments behind. Another breathless servant found my husband as he stood reeling from the losses of life and livestock. He had narrowly escaped to bring us the news that ripped my heart from my chest.

Within a matter of minutes, the horror of horrors was unleashed. He told of a great windstorm that had killed all ten of our children at once. They were gathered for a feast when the windstorm collapsed the tent upon them, and all were dead. Losing a child is every mother's worst nightmare. Losing all your children at once is unbearable and incomprehensible. All my children were gone!?!? The entirety of my life crashed at once!

I could not rest or cry. There was so much to do and process. I began mindlessly sifting through our belongings to try and find useful remnants. I was straining to comfort Job and understand the vastness of the losses we had suffered. The grief and duty were heavy and burdensome. There was no time to mourn before everyone began to talk. How could they dare say this was our fault or his sin? It made me angry and bitter, but Job was still praising God.

Job's obedience and faith were questioned by our community. It felt like our position and place in society were also being robbed from us. It brought great shame. Everyone believed we had sinned; that Job, my righteous husband, had broken God's commandments and the laws. I tried to remain strong, but it was too much. Why didn't they just help us instead of judging us?

On top of it all, Job became sick. In the midst of all the terror, he fell gravely ill. Imagine watching the one you love—the one who had fathered your now dead children—become sick and suffer. He agonized through such a great illness that it distorted his appearance. The distortion was so disfiguring that even his friends did not recognize him anymore. He sat outside by a fire and scraped his sores with broken bits of clay pots. Sometimes I could hear him talking to God. My mind, body, and spirit were fragile and worn. I tried, I really tried.

I knew what he had undergone and endured. I began begging at the city gate for help. They kept saying it was hidden sin. Job said God was still worthy of praise. Maybe He was testing him. I was confused, scared, and angry. Sorrow and darkness had enveloped my household. My mind and words rambled. It was all so intensely complicated and difficult to grasp.

Why, God? I just want to understand why! What had we done to deserve this?

Would I lose him too? Would my husband die? I wandered into the field by the fire and saw him there. He looked weak and feeble. I snapped. I do not know what happened on that exact day, but I could not face it any longer. I screamed:

> *"Do you still hold fast your integrity?*
> *Curse God and die."*
> (Job 2:9b)

After all we had lost, I still could not even hold my husband and find comfort in his arms. I feared he might die, and I would lose him too. I would be left widowed and penniless, and the talk of the town. Why had God not seen our great love which had produced so much good? Why had God estranged me from relief and security? Why were my children taken before me? Why did He not hear my prayers or care for me? Why had He cast us aside?

Even as Job sat in ashes and mourned, he knew I was wrong. His body was riddled with boils which brought incredible pain. We were left with no money, no home, no children, and yet he clung to hope. Despair and devastation followed by loneliness, fear, and humiliation led me to words I would later regret, but not my Job. He remained God's man through each trial.

My husband responded by telling me I was speaking like a foolish woman. He reminded me all we had was given by God and could thus be taken back by God. (Job 2:10) I was being too emotional to understand it. I walked away and left him there with God. Job would later tell me how God had shown him his humble place in this world.

My husband rebuked me and reminded me of my place, but his words were not as harsh as they could have been. He did not call me foolish; he called my words foolish. It was his way of reminding me that no matter what, God was to be honored in his home, in our home. I disappointed him, myself, and God that day.

After a while, I came to understand he was right. I never fully understood why we had to experience all the trials, but I did understand His sovereignty. God eventually delivered us out of the cosmic chaos. Peace was restored. Rest came, and Job was completely healed. Ultimately, we were fully restored.

We went on to have more children and live in more abundance than before the incidents. Even though I had told my husband to rage against God and die, I reaped the benefits of restoration alongside him.[32] He had not sent me away or divorced me.

Broken, yet mended. Surely, I have stood wishing I could take back my words spoken out of hurt and haste. I am Job's wife and I ask you to learn the lessons you need from the story of my worst days.

Girls, the truth is, at a time when Job's wife should have been supporting him and helping him heal, she failed. Not just a stumble but a fall from grace, according to many historians. She sinned greatly and yet she was not struck dead. She was shown grace by God Himself as well as her husband. Grace is the unmerited favor of God. I implore you to learn the hard lessons and accept the free gifts of salvation, mercy, and grace, today.

For more information on Job's wife, read Job 2:9-10, 19:17 and 31:10.

REAL BATTLES: So Many Words

Kindness in today's world is not always our first thought, or our second thought for that matter. Our world is full of noise, opinions, and social media feeds with rapid-fire comebacks. We are fast to speak and slow to listen. We almost look for ways to be easily offended. Some look for ways to be offensive and rude as if it is a joke. The mindset where "humor" cuts to the quick and puts someone else down in the process is warped. It seems that kindness is often in short supply.

In 2019, a scientific journal noted a study conducted in Western and Eastern countries with a large sampling population. By far, the most sought-after trait in a lifelong mate, by both sexes, was kindness. According to the study, kindness was chosen above physical attractiveness, finances, humor, and a host of other qualities as the most important characteristic.[33] This intrigues me.

If we desire kindness so desperately, then why don't we use it more liberally ourselves? Anger and impatience spill into tone, speech, actions, and attitude. I am the worst at times. I want people to be incredibly patient with me, but I am not always great at being patient with others. I get paid to speak, so listening must be intentional for me.

I have literally had business conversations where people think I am mad when I am not. I am very direct with my tone and my manner in business meetings. I hear phrases like, "You don't sugar coat things, do you?" No, I do not, but I certainly never mean to offend or intimidate others into action.

As a woman representing Christ, I want to become more like the description in Colossians:

> *"Put on then, as God's chosen ones, holy and beloved,*
> *compassionate hearts, kindness,*
> *humility, meekness, and patience."*
> (Colossians 3:12)

My speech and language, as well as my body language and facial gestures, impact how others hear what I say. Much research exists surrounding eye contact, enunciation, and how a closed body position such as arms folded versus an open position, impacts how others perceive our words.

"Choose kind words" and "fix your face" are two phrases I use frequently. They are reminders about words and facial expressions to myself and to those around me. I am ashamed of myself in this area at times. I still need lots of practice.

I taught sixth graders for many years and sometimes I speak to grown adults with the same tone of voice. It is rarely received well and then I must apologize and regroup. A few years back, I did an impromptu roasting of a youth director at a summer camp event. The room laughed many times. But, at some point, my picking became too much. I hurt this guy whom I love like a brother and offended some of his teens.

After I apologized to him, I told him I would come apologize in person to his people. He declined my offer because he was okay, but if our roasting someone by picking on them or teasing them is funny to us or the crowd, but not to the person we are teasing, is it funny at all? Maybe it is bullying. Words matter.

REAL POWER FOR THE REAL WORLD: The Kindness Challenge

We often look at the story of Job only from the perspective of what Job suffered and endured. It is taught through the lens of how God tested him and what the enemy brought against him. It's a hard story with twists and turns. It is complicated and difficult for us to understand. We wonder why Job had to endure so much. Why was he a central figure in a battle of good versus evil?

Many Christians struggle with why God would allow such a test and give the enemy permission. Yet, we are still learning valuable lessons from it today. In the midst of the story, we find one little part; Job 2:9. This verse holds ten words that have caused disdain and scorn for Job's wife, for centuries. Augustine labeled her "the devil's accomplice." Calvin called her "a diabolical fury."[34]

Only Heaven knows the truth of her spirit. But there are lessons for us to learn through her eyes and actions. Words matter, even in the heat of a tragedy. They matter to our spouses, children, co-workers, friends, and even to acquaintances. Kind words can have a lasting impact. Although there is some debate, most attribute this quote to Mother Teresa, "Kind words can be short and easy to speak, but their echoes are truly endless."[35]

When God changes our heart, the inner spirit becomes more in line with His will and ways, and kindness can overflow out of love. Love for

Him and love for those He loves brings kindness and softer words into our toolbox.

> *"She opens her mouth with wisdom,*
> *and on her tongue is the law of kindness."*
> (Proverbs 31:26 NKJV)

I challenge all of us to be intentionally kind with our words. Accept the challenge, then document the outcome of your interactions. Kind words can change someone's day or week—maybe even more. Be the change you want to see when it comes to kindness and word choices. Here are some ideas:

- Find a hard worker, who may often be overlooked, and speak kindness and appreciation.
- Look for someone whom others may shun and speak kindly to them.
- Offer a frazzled mom words of encouragement.
- Write a note of appreciation to your pastor.
- Send a card to nursing home residents who were public servants, military, or emergency workers, thanking them for their service.
- Send one of your former teachers a thank you or an email explaining their impact on your life.

Honestly, I would love to hear your stories once you have completed the challenge.

Get Real: Prayer & Reflection

1. How has someone surprised you with an act of kindness?

2. What is something kind you enjoy doing for others and how can you intentionally do it this week?

3. What can you learn from the story of Job's wife?

4. Write a memory of kind words spoken to you by a parent, grandparent, sibling, teacher, pastor, or friend. How did they impact you or the trajectory of your life? How can you use them to help someone else?

5. With whom or in what situation do you struggle with kind words most, and why?

6. What can you do to be purposeful in working on your kindness with the people or situations in question five?

7. What were the results of your Kindness Challenge?

Father God,

I pray my life will never have to be tested as Job's was. Help me to learn the lessons You have for me from reading and taking the story to heart, instead of having to live it myself. I ask for my family to remain safe and healthy. I ask for protection against the enemy's attacks and for Your presence to be known.

In Jesus' name,

Amen.

CHAPTER 13

Listening Takes Patience

*"And we urge you, brothers, admonish the idle,
encourage the fainthearted, help the weak, be patient with them all."*
(I Thessalonians 5:14)

REAL LIFE: How Long Does It Take?

How can the lack of a single character trait cause such a multitude of issues? Lack of patience causes so much conflict within us and within the world around us. We live in an age where instant gratification pushes us to want everything NOW. Waiting for any length of time stresses us out. If you have watched people stand in line, it is obvious even a five-minute wait is a major inconvenience.

Waiting at a traffic light or in a line causes people to bang on their steering wheels and honk their horns if the first car does not gun it when the light changes. Grown adults throw tantrums like two-year-old children when they are inconvenienced by waiting. Holding the hand of an actual two-year-old, as they walk a long hallway, seems to take an eternity. Instead, we scoop them up and run off. They lose practice time because we lose patience.

P-A-T-I-E-N-C-E is hard for many and nearly impossible for some.

Lack of patience when listening to opposing viewpoints is seen daily during live broadcasts and on social media. Can we try to understand what opposing sides are saying without dismissing or hating one another anymore? We have no time to hear someone who does not agree with us. We say things like, "They don't get it," or, "That's just stupid." Frustration, anger, abusive language, and hatred are far from Christ's teachings. If we are to be new creations in Christ, lessons on patience with all peoples must be learned and practiced.

Barbara Erochina wrote, "Patience is only needed when there is a reason to not wait. It is only necessary in the face of opposition." [36] If this is a true statement, then patience is the center of a battlefield where we muster endurance and strength for victory. It is also a place where we need God to show up and show off. Without His presence we will fall short.

We need a divine touch of His fingerprint on our heartbeat. His touch can slow our pulse and keep our blood pressure steady. Without it, our emotions and feelings may overrun our restraint during the battle. When we lose our temper, we say and do things we do not mean and cannot take back. When we become frustrated, we lose our peace.

It's an age-old human condition. David cried out in the desert, "How Long, oh Lord…" (Psalm 13). The same David who killed the giant Goliath grew weary of waiting for what he knew he was promised. As a child, David was anointed by God's messenger, Samuel. He was told he would become the King. That said, David was thirty years old before he was crowned King over all of Israel.

You would think that after being anointed as king, life would have been easy for him, but it wasn't. David faced hard battles and made huge mistakes. He hid in caves in the wilderness and was opposed by those whom he loved. Yet, God was faithful to him and He will be faithful to us; sometimes we just have to practice patience, wait, and listen.

When God is moving giants, climb up onto the watch tower, pray, and be still.

> *"I will take my stand at my watchpost*
> *and station myself on the tower and*
> *look out to see what he will say to me,*
> *and what I will answer concerning my complaint."*
> (Habakkuk 2:1)

REAL WOMEN FROM SCRIPTURE: EVE

I was the only woman in history to have no mother. I was created by the hand of God Himself. Holiness crafted me. My birth was a divine rendering made by God's fingertip pulled out of Adam's rib. We are all created for a purpose, but my purpose was evident from the moment God helped me take in breath. I am Eve and I was created to be the helpmate for the first human, Adam. I am called the mother of "all living."

I was woman, wife, mother, helper; lovely and sinless, until I made a fatal error. My sin is known by all and many have suffered because of it. What do you call it? Was it a temptation, greed, rebellion, or something else?

Maybe it was all of these, but my sin caused the downfall of the garden. It was the most beautiful and lovely place to live. We had freedom to linger and enjoy His magnificent creations. We played and lived in harmony with the animals. When I close my eyes tightly, I can still remember the perfection. If I focus, I can hear the sounds and smell the fragrances of freshness. Life was easy then, joy and plenty overflowed.

Now, we live in a broken and sin-filled world. Fear and evil voices surround us all the time. I hear the hiss of noise and know that because of my choices, death and destruction were brought into our family and the world. It is hard to sleep sometimes, because I can still hear the clamorous lies and pride filled taunts that entered the garden, too. They ring loudly in my ears.

Whispers were from the evil one, Satan. The serpent liar told me I had been tricked by God. Satan's forked tongue flattered me. He told me I could be smarter, wiser, more powerful, and full of all knowledge. He claimed God was withholding good from us.

Why had I been so easily fooled? Why had I even remained to listen? Why didn't I run away to immediately tell God what had happened? Why had I brought Adam to the abyss of evil? Why didn't he stop me? Why had he eaten the fruit too? I ask myself these questions and ten thousand more through toil, sweat, pain, and turmoil.

My choices…

My choices impacted us, the animals, the trees, and birds of the air. My choices impacted those we would grow to love; those who became our family. My choices brought destruction. My choices devastated. My choices blamed and shamed, they tore and obliterated.

I have learned what sin is. I have learned what a burden is. I have learned what wickedness is. I have learned that sin always has consequences.

God gave Adam and me every single thing in the garden with one exception. He warned us to stay away from the tree of the knowledge of good and evil. It was the one tree He told us not to eat fruit from. We had everything else. Everything we could have possibly ever wanted for and yet, I somehow thought it was not enough. Oh, that my days could be spent seeking forgiveness and harmony in my spirit…

I bore many consequences for my sin. Humanity was cursed as we fell.[37] I clearly remember that last day in perfection and long for its sweetness. I also know I was the first woman to cry pain-filled tears because I grieved my Creator, God. I was the first woman to have my eyes opened to all the damage my actions had caused. I was the first to understand the full meaning of guilt, shame, and regret. I've often wondered what would have happened, if…

But what I have yet to fully understand is the powerful depth of redemption and God's abundant mercy. I am Eve, and I am sorry.

Girls, the command God gave Adam and Eve is still applicable, in some ways, to us today. At times, I must ask myself am I eating from this evil sin-wrapped tree? I love knowledge. I want to know the answers to complex issues. I want to understand.

At this stage in my life, I know enough now to not pick rotten, evil fruit, but I still pick *good* knowledge fruit. Should I turn around and look at all the other trees in the garden instead? Maybe they are the trees of peace, the trees of joy, the trees of trusting, or the trees of faith. Wouldn't these be the trees God wants me to choose?

There is so much entangled in the story of Eve. I could not bring myself to write it from her perspective upon first submission of this book. It is still too big for me to fathom what she endured and helped cause by the sins of her own flesh. Yet, I have included this touch on her because I believe there are valuable questions which we need to ask ourselves as we look at her story. The cosmic battle of good versus evil is still real and our actions in it still impact generations of those we love.

For more on Eve, read Genesis 2-3, and II Corinthians 11:3.

REAL BATTLES: Waiting is Not a Game

In 2016, I wrote this in my journal: "I must become as good in the waiting as I am in the receiving." Why did I write this sentence? Waiting is not my greatest virtue. However, I want to have ears to listen for God's appointments and eyes to see His miracles. If I rush ahead of Him, I would be settling for my definition of great. I know His will always be greater than mine.

By its clinical definition, a miracle is a God thing, not a me thing. I cannot create my own miracles and perfect solutions; He must be in it for it to be a true miracle. Learning the simple truth of the saying "God is God, and I am not," may be harder than it seems for some of us.

As a general rule, many Americans are not good listeners. We multitask and are easily distracted during conversations. As an executive coach, working with leadership and management teams, I often ask how much more could be accomplished with ten minutes of authentic listening than inside a 30-60-minute meeting where no one is paying full attention.

We want to interrupt, ask questions, interject ideas, and formulate our own rebuttals instead of being present in the moment. Imagine what it would look like to someone if you put down the phone, stopped working on the computer, and turned to face them while simply listening.

Listening to the entire issue without solving it or jumping to conclusions can actually make the conversation go faster in the long run. I confess, the first time I took a listening test during my early coaching, I was so incredibly bad at it that my score was lower than the scale options. I was lower than the index of a "poor listener". That propelled me into the science of listening. Learning to listen has been a long quest. I expect it to be a lifetime of work.

This can also happen when I try to fix things God wants control over. I am stealing His power and authority in my life. I am not God. I cannot and should not try to solve or fix everything. If I can do something without Him, it is not a God sized prayer. I just need to get it done if I have the ability. But when the situation is incredibly difficult, and I keep trying to solve it by myself, I waste time and energy. I am also not depending upon God as I should.

When I was in my twenties, I took a bunch of high schoolers to a youth retreat. I heard a missionary there discuss how he wanted to pray *huge* prayers that made God look up and say, "What?" He talked about how he imagined God just listening to everyone talking at the same time, while simultaneously answering prayers and saving countries. He described himself praying a prayer *so big* God just stopped, smiled, and really paid attention.

There is a great deal in the illustration for theologians to argue, but I still remember the mental picture, decades later. I want to pray big prayers, be still and listen, and teach others how to do the same thing for themselves. Like Eve, I will miss God's miracles and blessings, then cause myself and others to fall when I do not pay attention to God's instructions.

REAL POWER FOR THE REAL WORLD: Is It God or Is It Me?

There have been times in my life when I feel like God is being quiet. They are some of the hardest, most difficult times for me. I know some people may not understand how God "talks" or how you can hear Him, but God does speak to us. He speaks through His Word, through others, and, if we are Christians, He speaks through His Holy Spirit.

In the past, there were many ways God spoke to His people. Through prophets, like Samuel and Daniel, He sent word to His people. Joseph was able to interpret dreams. Noah, Moses, Abraham, and others heard God speak to them directly. God sent Jesus to speak and teach His people. Elijah heard God as a "still small voice" (I Kings 19:11-13). And today, He is still the God of miracles. He still speaks and we can still hear Him if we know His voice (John 10:10, 27) and have discernment.

One of the questions I often get from women is, "How do I know it is God and not myself or the enemy?" My pastor teaches this in a simple three check process:

- God will never contradict himself so it will be Biblical.
- It will be how God hardwired you, even if it is uncomfortable.
- It will always serve a Kingdom purpose.

Let's look at these a bit more closely. First, God will never tell you something that goes against Scripture. For example, God is not going to tell us it is okay to have sex before marriage or commit adultery, even if we really love someone. There are numerous books of the Bible that teach on sexual immorality. We don't like this because sex has become more common than sacred. Sometimes we want to find a way to rationalize our sin, but we cannot pick and choose the scriptures we agree with to make our own Bible.

Secondly, I can use discernment and make sure that what I am hearing is coming from God by examining my hardwiring. God may ask me to do things that appear "crazy" to the world, but I can still do it if He is with me. He will give me the gifts, tools, skills, talents, and abilities to do what He is asking me to do, even if it stretches me considerably. An extreme example I use is that God will not wake me up tomorrow and put a burning desire in me to become a professional linebacker. I cannot do this even though I love football. I am not hardwired with anything that makes me capable of achieving this. So, it would not be a God idea for me.

Lastly, God will never ask us to do something that benefits us more than it does His Kingdom. There are times when we pray things for ourselves and we wonder if we are praying out of selfish gain. Check yourself for the fruit that can be grown out of the prayer. If you want a new vehicle and are praying for God to provide it or a way for it, are you willing to use it for Kingdom purposes? If we hoard God's blessings, we rob His Kingdom.

Use discernment and check what you are hearing from God against these three things. If He is being silent, wait. Repent if needed. Refine your prayers to make sure they align with Him and be patient. We have no idea what mountains He is moving behind the scenes. God's timing is not our timing, but He is always on a Heavenly schedule and it's better than ours.

Get Real: Reflection & Prayer

1. Why is it so difficult to be patient when God makes us wait?

2. What have patience and impatience led to in your life?

3. When is it hardest for you to obey what is right?

4. What was a new idea for you around the story of Eve?

5. What or who do you need to give to God in prayer and let Him have control over for the miracle?

6. What was a new idea for you in, Is it God or is it me?

7. Write out Psalm 40:1.

Father God,

I ask that You bless my mouth and ears to hear and listen as You see fit in every situation. Help me to be patient and present in conversations. Give me the ability to hear others as much as I want to be heard. Have Your way in my life, God. I submit to Your authority for the answers.

In Jesus' name,

Amen.

CHAPTER 14

A Scarlet Thread Leads to Redemption

"The Spirit of the Lord God is upon me, because the Lord has anointed me to bring good news to the poor; he has sent me to bind up the brokenhearted, to proclaim liberty to the captives, and the opening of the prison to those who are bound; to proclaim the year of the Lord's favor, and the day of vengeance of our God; to comfort all who mourn; to grant to those who mourn in Zion— to give them a beautiful headdress instead of ashes, the oil of gladness instead of mourning, the garment of praise instead of a faint spirit; that they may be called oaks of righteousness, the planting of the Lord, that he may be glorified."
(Isaiah 61:1-3)

REAL LIFE: Do Overs

One of my favorite terms is "scarlet thread." For me, it represents Christ's blood sacrifice being woven through His story of my life. His blood binds me to Him and makes my story His story. I have a scarlet thread of redemption that runs from March 16, 2012 to March 8, 2020. I did not know it was being woven by God's hand.

Have you ever seen someone working on a needlepoint piece, or sewing something inside out? The threads on the back or the inside can look like a disjointed mess at times, but when the piece is turned over and facing right side out, there is an amazing picture or a beautiful garment.

That had to be what my life looked like. From my perspective, things were a mess. The pieces did not fit together correctly or tightly for years. There were gaps and holes in my life's tapestry. I could not figure out what was missing or how to fill them in with my earthly vision.

God is always faithful to pull us close and keep working on us. He will make sure His creation comes together in more intricate and stunning ways than we could ever imagine. Even when we know He is at work, there are times when we still cannot see it. We feel like we are supposed to be doing something and maybe, somehow, we have missed it. Trust. God will not let you accidently miss what He has for you.

It was just like any other weekend. I was blessed to be helping lead worship on our platform and going about my normal duties as a staff member. Bryan and I had been dating for several months. Honestly, I was a bit upset with him that morning, so I was listening to funny videos as I worked. Since our dating was often long-distance, one of our rules was spending a minimum of fifteen minutes video chatting each day. He had blown me off the day before and my feelings were hurt.

We had phone conversations, but they were brief. He was busy at work then had to drive three hours for a dinner meeting with someone. His last message to me explained he was just too tired after his long day. I asked him to video chat long enough to at least say goodnight, but he declined. In all the months we had been together, it was the first day I had not seen his face.

Little did I know he was lying to me. Bryan was actually in town and had picked up a beautifully crafted one-of-a-kind ring for me the day before. I had no idea he was going to make a surprise appearance and propose. That Sunday morning, God began to cinch the broken threads and make our tapestries come together.

My pastor, Spencer, and my creative friend, Dixie, set it all up. Bryan had flown in, gotten a hotel room, picked up my ring from the jeweler, eaten at one of our favorite spots, and talked to me from a rental car in the church parking lot. I had been clueless about all of it.

After our church service, there are always announcements and a closing prayer from the platform. Dixie had texted me Saturday night and asked me to do a ministry highlight and promote our event for kiddos with special needs. It was late, but it was also nothing too unusual. Each staff member promoted their upcoming ministry opportunities and events as needed. So, I did not think too much about it.

Clearly, I was absolutely in the dark about the whole plan because I showed up in jeans, a t-shirt and an oversized sweater. I did not even get my heels out of the car, which is unusual for me. During the first service, the announcements and promotion went easily and was well received. But after second service, Dixie intentionally made me shift spots, to be in-between she and Spencer.

If you knew them, you would understand why one might be concerned in this position. They are savvy and sassy, so you must be on your toes. It is always good fun, but you never know what might happen. After I finished my spiel, things got weird. Dixie started playing with my hair and Spencer apologized to me while we were all still standing in the middle of the platform.

Spencer began talking about how much he and the staff love me. He mentioned how it had been an honor to watch me work with our ministries and be able to walk me through my long journey of widowhood. None of this had happened after first service, so I was trying to process what was occurring. I tried to look around to see what was going on, but Dixie was blocking me from turning my head as she played with my hair.

I looked down to the front row, and my friend Clarissa had slid from her family on the side to the seat right in front of me. It was odd, because she had one of the cheesiest grins I had ever seen on her face. Then, she raised up her phone. Spencer was still talking. He made a point about trusting God to heal our greatest hurts. He had told a bit of my background and then he noted that today there was more to the story.

At that point, Dixie stepped back, and I saw Bryan coming out from the side of the platform. To say I was stunned speechless is no exaggeration. I just began weeping uncontrollably and stomping my feet. I was a mess! I am talking, mascara down my white shirt, snot running down my face, ugly crying, mess! Dixie was jumping up and down and everyone was cheering.

Oh, my heart!

Bryan came towards me and hugged me tightly. He looked much more prepared and composed than I did. He spoke some of the most elegant words about what we had lost and what God was giving us as a second chance together. His words were filled with power and his voice was steady and calm. I was blubbering. Then he dropped to one knee and asked me to marry him.

Somewhere in there I may have told him I was going to punch him in the face, but I was lying…I hugged him hard, stomped some more, and shook my head, "Yes." Dixie had helped stage an EPIC surprise proposal for me. As the Executive Director of Daryl's Music Makers, she had seen my brokenness redeemed through our foundation work and then through a new journey of healing and hope.

That day, my tribe all loved me well. After months of behind-the-scenes planning, a scarlet thread was pulled tight. Bryan had used people who loved me to craft one of the most beautiful surprises of my life. He took a comment I had made about his ability to keep surprises secret to a whole new level. About three hours later, after a meeting over lunch with our staff and the church leaders, we decided to go ahead and get married. No need to wait when you know God had it planned all along. That day, I got a new name, and an epic redemption story whose ending is still being written.

REAL WOMEN FROM SCRIPTURE: RAHAB

Can you explain to me another way a single woman was to make money in a town with little need or desire for a sovereign God? I am known, by many, as "Rahab the Prostitute."[38] There was and still is much more to me than this title, but people did not always care. I am not sure how I came to the "profession" other than I was hungry and husbandless. Maybe it was because of rebellion or rejection, I cannot remember. It was all so long ago.

I recall people judging me harshly as I went about my business. I had all the food and money I needed. I even had my own house on the outskirts of town. I could not live too closely to others because it would have deterred some of my visitors.

In those days, our town stayed busy with many travelers. They loved to tell stories as they came and went. Nobody stayed put for too long. My house was situated on the back wall of our fortified city, which made it a bit easier for them to enter and exit discreetly. My roof was high but the visitors who secretly climbed it were many. Travelers from abroad were not the only visitors. Men who had wives and high positions in town also came to me in the darkness.

Sometimes they sought refuge and rest. Sometimes they sought my body for pleasures. Yet, at other times, they sought my ears to listen to their adventures and bloody battles. They wanted to tell their stories. Stories that marked them as hunters, heroes, and great warriors. I have always listened well. It is an important asset.

Some called it a dangerous job, but I felt safe and protected most days. My home's location was near the city gate and built into a thick fortification wall. But the time came when this was not the case. There was no protection to be found inside my mind and spirit. For years, I had heard the stories of the army of Israel from my traveling guests. The stories of these people and their God have long caused fear here in our city and wonder in my imagination.

I have heard tales that these Israelites had defeated the Egyptians by walking through the Red Sea upon dry ground. Can you imagine the heavens making water part to provide safe passage for hundreds of thousands, and then swallowing up those who hunted them down? It was told that the warriors of Israel had defeated the great Amorite Kings and won many other impressive battles. They were mighty and powerful. Their God protected them and gave them victories that should not have been theirs.

I did not understand it all, because I had not yet seen it firsthand. But, when I heard stories of unusual and mighty victories over and over, I began to believe their truth. It seemed to me that the God of Israel was impressive. He certainly was more present and dependable than the worthless gods worshipped in our culture. I had not seen anything come from them. We were tossed about not knowing what would cause our prayers to be answered. So many choices and no results.

The stories told and retold by mere men and warriors alike, of the God of Israel, were different. I had heard them spoken by men who wanted to brag and boast, and men who wanted to run and hide. This deity was real. Nothing else could explain the tales, aside from a real God.

Even though I had grown up in a city that worshiped many gods, had I somehow come to wonder and believe in the God of Israel? Our city, Jericho, was a city of fools. It was filled with idol worship,[(39)] wickedness, and large men who loved to fight, but not understand the heavens. Yet, there were many beautiful things in Jericho. We were a city where milk and honey flowed, and where fruit was bountiful. It was a land that others wanted, especially the men of Israel.

In some ways, I had protected it before. I had been okay with our way of life.

But when two Israelites showed up at my door, I knew it was time to make a change. I should have panicked, but something about them captured me on the inside. I have good intuition. I knew when those at my door were dangerous. These men were not, even though they were on the run. It was as if they were under a different authority. They had presence and purpose. In the blink of an eye, I knew I was willing to risk everything for their mission on the God of Israel's behalf.

"Come, come quickly!" I said, my pulse racing. News had always traveled fast in my neighborhood; I knew the King's men were after these two. What had possessed me to betray our land and lie to the king's men? I knew if I was caught, I would have been killed. The only way I can explain it is that I just knew, somewhere in the depths of my being, their God was what I needed. I wanted to know Him. If he killed the mighty Egyptians that chased their people, He would help save me.

I rushed to hide them on my roof under drying flaxseed stalks as quickly and quietly as possible. I knew it would not be long before the king's guardsmen arrived. They would follow orders. If they found any reason to suspect I was hiding invaders, it would have been the end of me. It would have also been the end of the two men of God for spying on Jericho and trying to return word to their army.

Lots of things happened inside those walls but murdering those men could not be added to the list. I could not allow it to happen in my house. Each time I looked at them, I could see the power that came with them. They held truth and served a God I longed to know. They were my way out. He is my way out!

"Quickly, quickly!" I had beckoned as I hid them under the weight of the harvested flax. I whispered, "Be quiet, stay buried. Do not move. Shhhh, please! They are coming." I raced back down the stairs to gain my composure before I opened the door.

The pounding of my heart was so loud I feared the guardsmen might be able to hear it.

BANG! BANG! BANG! Came the knocks upon the door, in rapid succession.

The king's men were shouting, "Open up, let us in!" I took a breath, looked down to brush off any flax from my garments, then answered the door. The next words I spoke betrayed my people but would somehow rescue humanity.

I measured my words carefully and calmly. I told the guards the men had come and gone through the city gate just as it closed around dark. Then I raised my voice and urged them to run after the spies. I convinced them if they left quickly enough, they would catch up with the two men and overtake them (Joshua 2:4-6).

They hesitated, "Go." I yelled, "GO!"

It worked, they left.

I went back up to the roof and made a pact with the spies, who were men of God. I traded their safety for the safety of my own family and those I loved. My house sat on the outer walls of Jericho. Little had I known those walls that had protected me for so long were about to come tumbling down. What I did know, was because of our pact, my family would be protected when the invading army arrived.

They had left by climbing down a rope hung through my window over the rim of the outer city wall. Before they escaped, they had given me instructions to gather my family in my home on the day of their invasion. They promised as the siege came, none of us would be hurt. They had left me with a scarlet cord to hang outside my window. The cord was to be displayed as the sign of my alliance with the foreign army. If it was not visible, we would be killed.

My family had to be told, prepared, and gathered without drawing suspicion. They had heard the rumors, too, and had known the attack of Joshua's army was imminent. We collected some of our belongings as cunningly as we could. During those days, we tried not to draw undue attention. We had all gone about our daily lives as best we could. I suppose I should have been more afraid of being caught, but I had felt a veiled protection in it all.

It was the strangest battle any of us would ever witness. The army came and surrounded our city, but they did not attack right away. There was no yelling or speaking we could hear, only the sound of battle horns. [40] On the first day the army arrived, they had marched around the city early in the morning. We had heard the trumpets, but then they went back to their camp. They had marched with some men in battle gear, some only carrying horns, and some who appeared to be priests carrying a golden box. My family and I would later learn the holy significance of this box they called the arc of the covenant.

Our army and fighting men argued about what to do. Should they run out of the city to attack or stay put inside the walls, prepare, and let the battle come to them? Horns could not hurt the city, right? They determined to stay within the city's shelter and vigilantly watch for men to breach the walls; that would signal the real battle had begun. Day two, day three…for six days, there was no breach. We watched them just marching exactly as they had the day before and heard their trumpets blow.

On day seven, I knew the time had come. The army of Israel began their march at dawn. The trumpets pierced through the final moments of darkness as the moon set and the sun began its rise.

They continued to march. Once, twice, three times…

My family had gathered and all those I loved were in the house.

Four times…

I had thrown the scarlet cord out the window. We were ready.

Five times… the noise inside the city had built all morning.

Jericho knew the day of battle had arrived. The feeling in the air changed.

Six times… and then…

On the seventh march around the city, we heard the shouting!

It was a shout of triumph as if the battle had already been won. Then we felt the shaking of buildings and fortified walls collapsing. The army burst forth and plundered the city. The sounds were frightening, but we were safe, my house and all who were in it, were still standing.

The two spies came and gathered us. They escorted us through the rubble of destruction into a new life. When the walls fell, "Rahab the Prostitute" became a title of my past. That day I got a fresh start. That day, the scales were removed from my eyes to the truth of the Living God.

My reputation is now one of bravery, in my new land. I am a wife and mother. I have birthed a kind, strong son named Boaz. Long ago, a scarlet rope carried me into a new world, and now I am forever changed. I have a new song. I am Rahab, and I am redeemed through faith in the God of Israel.

Girls, understand the place of Rahab in the history of the Israelites. King David was born through her lineage.[40] From his line came Jesus Christ of Nazareth, the Savior of the world. It is ironic how the man who erased sin and death through His divine sacrifice was birthed through a line of sinners. God will use whomever He pleases, not whomever the world thinks He should use. He gives chances to seekers and sinners alike. Redemption belongs to anyone who will trust and believe. We just have to be willing to accept His gift.

For more information on the redemption of Rahab, read Joshua 2:1-3, 6:17-25; Matthew 1:5, Hebrews 11:31 and James 2:25.

REAL BATTLES: Where is Your War?

The world has changed, and the battle has now pushed us to the front lines. War on, my friends, but make sure the battle you are fighting is one that really matters and not one that is wasting your energy and supplies. Wage war with God's tools and not your own flesh. His tools are always bigger and better than ours.

> *"For we are not fighting against flesh-and-blood enemies,*
> *but against evil rulers and authorities of the unseen world,*
> *against mighty powers in this dark world,*
> *and against evil spirits in the heavenly places."*
> (Ephesians 6:12)

Earth has, and has had, so many wars. Nations fight nations. People fight within their own nations, tribes and races fight against one another, genders fight, parents and children fight, families fight, and even churches fight. There is so much injustice, war, bloodshed, and so many, many tears.

Yet, I believe the ultimate wars are not for blood or money; they are for our minds, our peace, our joy, our fullness, our words, our time, our treasures, and our talents. Ephesians 6 tells us our real war is against evil. The enemy loves to spin God's Word. He loves to distract and help us waste our time. When we toil and worry, try to make our own miracles, and wrestle ourselves, we are upside down on how God intends us to live. God still chases after those who do not yet know Him, just as He did with Rahab. He still chases after those who have known him and strayed. He still chases His children because He is a good Father. Is He chasing after you?

I hope you continue to explore all the possibilities of what we can hear when we get real with ourselves, get real with God, shut our mouths to listen, open ourselves up to serve, and continually pray. I hope you will find the words are no less inspired now than when He prompted me so long ago. If it has inspired you to do something, do not procrastinate as I did when I first heard the Lord tell me to write. Do what He has called you to, right now.

I pray you have found a word that sits in your spirit and seeps into your soul like a thick soothing balm. I pray it penetrates deeply and heals from the inside out.

REAL POWER FOR THE REAL WORLD:
Satan Hates Us...But God

Satan also uses guilt to make us feel bad for asking God to bless us. We are not supposed to ask for too many good things, right? That is spoiled, selfish, unholy. Yet, James 4:2b-3 says, *"You do not have, because you do not ask. You ask and do not receive, because you ask wrongly, to spend it on your passions."* This means that we should ask with a spirit aligned to the Holy Spirit. As long as we ask with the right heart, our heavenly Father wants to bless us.

He wants us to align our hearts with His blessings and fullness of life. Do not misunderstand, He wants us to live full lives, not so we become hoarders of the good, but givers in His name. If God blesses you with good gifts—peace, joy, provision, money, mercy, love, grace—there are people around who desperately need them. They are starved for them, so hand them out freely knowing God will provide more.

Give and it will come back to you. It's a promise.[41] You don't receive blessings so that you can hide them, you receive them to give them and become blessed by both the receiving and the giving. Use discernment but be generous givers. We live in a world on fire, so give and serve until they ask why.

Share your stories of God. Share who you used to be, how you met Him, and who you are now. Tell everyone who has ears to ear how God has changed you. Tell your redemption story. They can argue theology, but they cannot argue with your testimony. It is yours to tell.

Get Real: Reflection & Prayer

1. When have you been surprised by God?

2. How well do you receive unexpected blessings from God? Is it hard to accept them from Him or through other people He places in your path?

3. Why her? Why was Rahab singled out? What qualities do you see in her story from the book of Joshua?

4. Would you be willing to risk everything in your life if God singled you out? How daring would you have to be and what might make you hesitate?

5. What is your scarlet thread of redemption? What has God brought you out of and protected you from?

6. Who do you need to share your story with and why are you waiting?

7. Write out your story using the following three prompts:

    - Who was I before Christ?
    - How did I meet Him?
    - Who am I now or how has my life changed?

Father God,

Thank You for redemption. Help me to seek You and know You more. Call me deeper into You. Let my greatest love story be with Jesus. May I see the lost and broken as You do and share my stories of Your love with them. May I tell them of my very real God. Soften my heart and halt my quick judgments. Help me to be a real girl who chases the lost down and if I stray, I humbly ask that You chase me down too.

In Jesus' name,

Amen.

CONCLUSION
Author's Notes

"Therefore, since we are surrounded by so great a cloud of witnesses, let us also lay aside every weight, and sin which clings so closely, and let us run with endurance the race that is set before us, looking to Jesus, the founder and perfecter of our faith, who for the joy that was set before him endured the cross, despising the shame, and is seated at the right hand of the throne of God."
(Hebrews 12:1-2)

If I Could Speak Directly to Hearts

Single Women

If I could speak to the hearts of women who are engaged or dating, I would remind you to go into a marriage and relationships being mindful of Who gives you your identity. True identity is never found in another human being, not even one we love. Identity is only found in Christ. Be whomever He calls you to be and worry much less about what others think.

Marrieds

If I could speak to the hearts of couples in a struggling marriage, I would remind you that better jobs and more money cannot save a marriage. Having children cannot save a marriage. But there are a few things that can save one. Learning healthy communication skills can save a rocky marriage. Hard work, dedication, respecting one another, remaining faithful to your vows, your partners, your ethics, and God. These are things that can save marriages.

Wives, if you are in a marriage that is struggling, circle back and be reflective about what you can fix within yourself. Once that work is underway, pray for your spouse to draw closer to God and work on themselves. Do not badger him, it helps nothing. *"It is better to live on a corner of a roof than to share a house with a nagging wife."* (Proverbs 21:9, NIV)

Parents

If I could speak into the hearts of parents and guardians, I would remind you the greatest gift your children will ever receive is growing up in a godly home with parents who love each other first and then their children. A good healthy marriage is built upon mutual respect and regard, amicable ways of dealing with conflict, fair fights, and love that places God before your spouse and your children.

If your kids or your spouse are more important than your relationship and love for God, you will run out of energy, and conflicts will arise. When your kids or your spouse become your focus, (what you worship or your idol), and time with God is replaced by people, you will stumble. We must make Him our priority in order to live our best lives for the Kingdom and our families.

Struggling Believers and Leaders

If I could speak into the hearts of struggling believers or worn-out church leaders, I would remind you that each of us are created for a purpose. We are here during this historical time period, placed and appointed by an intentionally purposeful Creator. You are here in this season because He needs you. Let your heart be broken by what breaks His. Then set out anew each day to make small changes in those He places around you. It is okay to be tired. It is not okay to stay tired forever. Rest in Him and then pray for revival in your own heart.

My Tribe of Real Girls

If I could speak into the hearts of real girls serving a real God, I would ask, "Do you think Jesus ever felt tired along the way? Were the expectations too much, the crowds too large or too demanding?"

Of course, He got tired. We have evidence. *"Very early in the morning, while it was still dark, he departed and went out to a desolate place and there he prayed."* (Mark 1:35) If we back up a few verses, we see Jesus preaching, casting out demons, healing a sick friend, and ministering to a city that showed up on His doorstep at sundown. That was one day in the life of Christ, so the next day He found some stillness.

We see this again after the death of John the Baptist in Mark 6:31-32, and again in Mark 4:35-40. He modeled rest for us many times and we are commanded to keep a Sabbath. When do we find rest, stillness, peace, and help through difficulties? You are not in this alone. It does not make you brave to carry everything by yourself.

We are certainly no more important than Jesus was, so it must be a cursed mindset and/or an enemy scheme that makes us enslave ourselves to busyness and perfectionism in the world, our families, our businesses, and in ministry. This is not what God intended. Being too busy, even with good things, is still a bad thing.

In Matthew 11:28-30 of The Message, it reads, *"Come to me. Get away with me and you'll recover your life. I'll show you how to take a real rest. Walk with me and work with me—watch how I do it. Learn the unforced rhythms of grace. I won't lay anything heavy or ill-fitting on you. Keep company with me and you'll learn to live freely and lightly."* Meditate on this, and see what God brings out for you.

If I could speak to those of you who are at the end of themselves, I would remind you I have been there too, just as many people in this world have been. Please, do not give up. Call for help if you are in real danger or need reinforcements. You are valuable. God will always give you a way out. He created you, and He remembers your name.

> *"For we are his workmanship, created in Christ Jesus for good works, which God prepared beforehand, that we should walk in them."*
> (Ephesians 2:10)

> *"Behold, I have engraved you on the palms of my hands...."*
> (Isaiah 49:16a)

I pray you have found a fresh touch and new hope through these pages.

All blessing, honor, and glory go to the Real God.

Shalom.

About the Author

Dr. Teri Cox-Meadows has a passion for empowering others to become their best selves. She travels as an international education consultant, author, musician, and speaker. Teri was a recent *Soriee' Magazine* Woman to Watch, a graduate of Leadership Arkansas' Class XIV, and a member of the Arkansas Women's Leadership Forum. She is the current communications trainer for several business management teams and a keynote speaker, both nationally and internationally, for organizations such as Rotary International, Delta Kappa Gamma International, Arkansas Blue Cross Blue Shield, Arkansas Regional Organ Recovery Association, LOPA, and MORA.

In the business sector, Dr. Cox-Meadows is a leadership consultant, executive coach, and a communications specialist. She is the founder of Daryl's Music Makers, a nonprofit organization providing hope and future for children abroad and stateside, through music and education. She also has a passion for living a healthy lifestyle and is part of the Life Vantage and Optavia families. These businesses allow her the opportunity to help people feel better mentally and physically.

Teri is part of a dynamic staff at ReNew Community Church. She counts it an honor and privilege to work alongside leaders and innovators from the various fields of education, faith, public and private sector businesses and non-profits, to engage and inspire people to reach for their highest potential. She can empower your group with an inspirational keynote, a critical conversation, or a session that leads to change. Whatever the call, the journey will be inspirational, fun and educational.

coxconsulting.org

Endnotes

1. Rosenburg, Jennifer. "A Short History of the Ball of Goo Called Silly Putty." *ThoughtCo.*, 31 January 2019, www.thoughtco.com/the-history-of-silly-putty-1779330. Accessed 7, September 2020.

2. *The Holy Bible.* English Standard Version, BibleGateway.com, https://www.biblegateway.com/passage/?search=James+1&version=ESV.

3. *The Holy Bible.* English Standard Version, BibleGateway.com, https://www.biblegateway.com/resources/all-women-bible/Zipporah.

4. Frymer-Kensky, Tikva. "Zipporah: Bible." 27 February 2009, Jewish Women's Archive, jwa.org/encyclopedia/article/zipporah-bible.

5. *GotQuestions.org.* https://www.gotquestions.org/life-Mary-Bethany.html. Accessed 14, July 2020.

6. *The Holy Bible.* English Standard Version, BibleGateway.com, https://www.biblegateway.com/passage/?search=John+11&version=ESV.

7. *BibleGateway.com.* "All Women of the Bible — Mary of Bethany." https://www.biblegateway.com/resources/all-women-bible/Mary-Bethany.

8. *The Holy Bible.* English Standard Version, BibleGateway.com, https://www.biblegateway.com/passage/?search=Mark+14&version=ESV.

9. *Goodreads.com.* www.goodreads.com/author/quotes/1032289.Dorothy_Neville_Rolfe. Accessed 9 September 2020.

10. *AnswersInGenesis.org.* https://answersingenesis.org/, 2020.

11. *GotQuestions.org.* https://www.gotquestions.org/Mary-Magdalene.html. Accessed 15, January 2017.

12. *BibleGateway.com.* "All Women of the Bible — Mary Magdalene." https://www.biblegateway.com/resources/all-women-bible/Mary-Magdalene.

13. *BibleGateway.com.* "All Women of the Bible — Lot's Wife." https://www.biblegateway.com/resources/all-women-bible/Lot-8217-s-Wife.

14. Kadari, Tamar. "Lot's Wife: Midrash and Aggadah." Jewish Women: A Comprehensive Historical Encyclopedia. 27 February 2009. Jewish Women's Archive, jwa.org/encyclopedia/article/lots-wife-midrash-and-aggadah.

15. "Faithful." *Dictionary.com*, 2020, www.dictionary.com/browse/faithful. Accessed 9, July 2020.

16. *BibleGateway.com.* "All Women of the Bible — Potiphar's Wife." https://www.biblegateway.com/resources/all-women-bible/Potiphar-8217-s-Wife.

17. *GotQuestions.org.* https://www.gotquestions.org/Potiphars-wife.html. Accessed 8, February 2018.

18. "Is Eudaimonia the Only Word for Happiness in Ancient Greek?". *Quora*, www.quora.com/Is-eudaimonia-the-only-word-for-happiness-in-ancient-Greek. Accessed 9, October 2020.

19. https://www.blueletterbible.org/lang/lexicon/lexicon.cfm?t=kjv&strongs=h833. Accessed 16, March 2020.

20. "5479. Chara." *Bible* Hub, biblehub.com/greek/5479.htm. Accessed 2, June 2020.

21. "1249. Diakonos." *Bible Hub*, biblehub.com/greek/1249.htm. Accessed 9, October 2020.

22. *BibleGateway.com*. "All Women of the Bible — Phebe, Phoebe." https://www.biblegateway.com/resources/all-women-bible/Phebe-Phoebe.

23. *GotQuestions.org*. https://www.gotquestions.org/Phoebe-in-the-Bible.html. Accessed 30, August 2018.

24. "People who were abused as children are more Likely to be abused as an adult." https://www.ons.gov.uk/peoplepopulationandcommunity/crimeandjustice/articles/peoplewhowereabusedaschildrenaremorelikelytobeabusedasanadult/2017-09-27. Accessed 16, July 2020.

25. *The Holy Bible*. English Standard Version, BibleGateway.com, https://www.biblegateway.com/passage/?search=Judges+13&version=ESV.

26. "Mother of Samson: Bible." *Jewish Women's Archive,* https://jwa.org/encyclopedia/article/mother-of-samson-bible.

27. *The Holy Bible.* English Standard Version, BibleGateway.com, https://www.biblegateway.com/passage/?search=Psalm+127&version=ESV.

28. *BibleGateway.com.* "Woman of Samaria." https://www.biblegateway.com/resources/all-women-bible/Woman-Samaria.

29. *GotQuestions.org.* https://www.gotquestions.org/woman-at-the-well.html. Accessed 7, December 2019.

30. Nield, David. "WATCH: Your Tears Are as Unique (And Beautiful) As Snowflakes." *Sciencealert.com*, 3 September 2016, www.sciencealert.com/your-tears-are-as-unique-andas-beautiful-as-snowflakes. Accessed 30, August 2020.

31. "Woman With Issue of Blood." *BibleGateway*, https://www.biblegateway.com/resources/all-women-bible/Woman-Issue-Blood. Accessed 3, September 2020.

32. *BibleGateway.com.* "Job's Wife." https://www.biblegateway.com/resources/all-women-bible/Job-8217-s-Wife.

33. Bergland, Christopher. "The Trait People Desire Most in a Partner." 20 September 2019, *PsychologyToday.com*, www.psychologytoday.com/us/blog/the-athletes-way/201909/the-trait-people-desire-most-in-partner. Accessed 14, July 2020.

34. *BibleGateway.com.* "Job's Wife." https://www.biblegateway.com/resources/all-women-bible/Job-8217-s-Wife.

35. *Goodreads.com.* https://www.goodreads.com/author/quotes/838305.Mother_Teresa. Accessed 14, July 2020.

36. Erochina, Barbara. "Practicing Patience When God Has You Waiting." *Thelife.com*. Rpt. in <u>Endingpovertytogether.org</u>. Cont. P2C Digital Strategies. Website. Accessed 4, July 2020.

37. *BibleGateway.com*. "All Women of the Bible — Eve." <u>https://www.biblegateway.com/resources/all-women-bible/Eve</u>.

38. *BibleGateway.com*. "All Women of the Bible — Rahab." <u>https://www.biblegateway.com/resources/all-women-bible/Rahab</u>.

39. *GotQuestions.org*. <u>https://www.gotquestions.org/life-Rahab.html</u>. Accessed 21, June 2017.

40. Frymer-Kensky, Tikva. "Rahab: Bible." *Jewish Women: A Comprehensive Historical Encyclopedia*. Accessed 27, February 2009. Jewish Women's Archive. <u>https://jwa.org/encyclopedia/article/rahab-bible</u>.

41. *The Holy Bible*. English Standard Version, BibleGateway.com, <u>https://www.biblegateway.com/passage/?search=Luke+6&version=ESV</u>.

Made in the USA
Columbia, SC
12 October 2024